Starting a Business Guide for Beginners in 2024:

Starting Strong as an Entrepreneur, Building and Sustaining a Successful Company with Ease and Confidence."

By

DARYL V. MEYER

Copyright

About the author

Welcome to the author's page, where passion meets practical wisdom in the realm of entrepreneurship. Daryl V. Meyer, a dedicated advocate for aspiring business owners, is on a mission to empower individuals with the fundamental knowledge needed to kickstart their entrepreneurial journey.

Daryl V. Meyer brings a wealth of experience and insight to the table, fueled by a genuine desire to assist others in realizing their dreams of starting and sustaining successful businesses. He understands the nuances of entrepreneurship and aims to demystify the process for those taking their first steps into the business world.

Driven by the belief that everyone has the potential to be a successful entrepreneur, Daryl V. Meyer is committed to providing accessible and practical guidance. His approach centers on delivering basic yet invaluable ideas, recognizing that a strong foundation is key to navigating the complexities of starting a business.

Through his writing, Daryl V. Meyer strives to simplify the entrepreneurial landscape, breaking down intimidating concepts into manageable, actionable steps. Whether you're a seasoned professional exploring a new venture or a budding entrepreneur with a vision, Daryl V. Meyer is here to offer a roadmap that fosters confidence and clarity.

With a writing style that balances expertise with approachability, Daryl V. Meyer is your companion on this exciting journey. Expect to find a treasure trove of insights, real-world examples, and hands-on advice that transcends the theoretical, guiding you through the essential aspects of entrepreneurship.

Daryl V. Meyer believes in the transformative power of entrepreneurship to shape lives and communities. By sharing foundational ideas and fostering a supportive environment, he envisions a landscape where individuals from diverse backgrounds can confidently pursue their entrepreneurial aspirations.

Whether you're flipping through these pages seeking guidance on business planning, market research, or simply drawing inspiration from Daryl V. Meyer's entrepreneurial journey, you're in capable hands. This author doesn't just offer knowledge; he extends an invitation to join a community of aspiring entrepreneurs, where questions are welcomed, and success is a shared celebration.

Embark on this journey with Daryl V. Meyer, and let the pages ahead be a source of inspiration and practical wisdom as you take the plunge into the exhilarating world of entrepreneurship. Your business adventure starts here.

Table of content

Introduction

Welcome to "Starting a Business Handbook for Novices 2024," your go-to asset for researching the enchanting excursion of business. We have separated the convoluted course of beginning a business into simple to-follow ventures for fledglings in this thorough aid. Whether you're a developing business visionary or someone serious to change into a productive undertaking, this book is expected to demystify the cycle, giving you a smoothed out guide for building a prospering association.

With the assurance that comes from a well-written business plan, efficient marketing strategies, and a solid comprehension of the essentials, set out on this adventure. We'll dive into the intricacies of legitimate thoughts, financing decisions, and the specialty of denoting, all while ensuring that the information is presented in an open way, great for new company individuals.

Prepare to find your beginning strength and open the ways to pioneering achievement. This isn't just a book; It is your manual for beating deterrents, enjoying triumphs, and, eventually, beginning a business that can go the distance. We ought to go on this trip together and make your dreams about starting another business a reality!

Overview of entrepreneurship

In the huge embroidery of business and development, business venture remains as a unique power that shapes economies, drives advancement, and engages people to transform dreams into the real world.This outline is an examination concerning the center of business — an outing that transcends standard work ways and invites individuals to become designers of their own destinies.

At its pith, business venture is the quest for open doors past the extent of customary work. It is tied in with perceiving the holes on the lookout, imagining effective fixes, and going ahead with well balanced plans of action to rejuvenate those arrangements. Money managers visionaries who view difficulties as meandering stones, not bars, and who embrace shortcoming as a material for development.

Fundamental to business is the soul of development. It's not only about beginning organizations; it's tied in with changing businesses, disturbing standards, and introducing positive change. This outline highlights the necessary job of imagination and ground breaking in business, featuring that the best endeavors frequently rise out of a readiness to rock the boat.

In excess of a bunch of abilities, business is an outlook — an approach to moving toward issues, immediately jumping all over chances, and exploring the eccentric idea of business.This layout dives into the key characteristics that portray an ambitious standpoint, including strength, flexibility, keenness, and the ability to change hardships into significant models.

Business venture is an excursion, set apart by particular stages from ideation to foundation and development. This layout offers encounters into each stage, giving a perception of the troubles and entryways that money managers experience in transit. From encouraging a business thought to scaling undertakings, the creative trip is a strong development with exceptional solicitations constantly.

Past individual pursuits, business ventures assume a significant part in molding economies and social orders. This diagram researches the greater impact of undertaking, underlining its obligation to work creation, monetary turn of events, and the improvement of innovative responses for social challenges. Business people are impetus for change, and their endeavors frequently swell a long way past the limits of their underlying yearnings.

Undertaking blooms with assortment, welcoming individuals from various establishments, social orders, and experiences. This outline perceives the significance of inclusivity in the pioneering biological system, featuring that a variety of viewpoints cultivates more extravagant development and guarantees that business venture is a space open to all.

As we finish up this outline of a business venture, think of it as a challenge to embrace the pioneering soul. Whether you're a carefully prepared entrepreneur, a hopeful startup lover, or somebody inquisitive about the universe of development, business venture offers an excursion of disclosure, versatility, and significant effect. Welcome to the energetic scene where thoughts prosper, and people try to shape their fates through the force of business venture.

Key qualities of a successful entrepreneur

Setting out on a pioneering venture isn't just about having a good thought; about typifying specific characteristics drives you toward progress. We ought to examine the key qualities that set thriving business visionaries to the side in the one of a kind universe of business.

• Visionary Thinking:

Effective business people have a sharp feeling of vision. They don't simply see the present; they imagine a future where their thoughts have changed into the real world. It's this earth shattering methodology that coordinates their decisions and stimulates their confirmation, allowing them to investigate troubles with an eye on the end-all strategy.

• Strength and Flexibility:

The way to progress is seldom smooth, and business visionaries experience misfortunes and difficulties. The capacity to return, gain from disappointments, and adjust to changing conditions is a sign of fruitful business people. Versatility pushes them along whenever troubles arise, guaranteeing they arise more grounded from each obstruction.

• Risk-Taking Boldness:

Business venture is innately connected with risk, and fruitful business visionaries won't hesitate to go ahead with reasonable courses of action. They comprehend that development frequently includes venturing outside the safe place, and they embrace the vulnerability that accompanies it. This boldness to face challenges is a main thrust behind earth shattering thoughts and adventures.

• Strong Work Ethic:

Building a successful business demands hard work and dedication. Business people who flourish are known for their steady hard working attitude. They're not afraid to put in the hours, sweat the details, and go the extra mile. This obligation to difficult work turns into the establishment whereupon their endeavors stand and develop.

• Effective Communication Skills:

Communication is at the foundation of entrepreneurship. Strong cash directors prevail with regards to articulating their vision, persuading partners, and building strong protections.Productive correspondence is a principal quality that prompts them forward, whether it's pitching to cash related help, driving a get-together, or helping clients.

• Adaptation to Change:

In the fast-paced business world, adaptability is non-negotiable. Effective business visionaries rush to embrace change, whether it's in innovation, market patterns, or buyer conduct. Their capacity to turn when important and remain on the ball guarantees that their endeavors stay applicable and versatile.

• Financial Savvy:

Fiscal wit is a critical skill for successful entrepreneurs. They handle the complex nuances of organizing, financial course of action, and assetallocating.This cash related splendid connects with them to pursue informed choices, examine fiscal dissonances, and evidence the genuine enhancement of their trials.

• Customer-Centric Focus:

Thriving entrepreneurs prioritize their customers. They keenly understand the needs and preferences of their target audience, using customer feedback to refine products or services. This client driven approach encourages steadfastness as well as positions their endeavors for long haul outcome in a cutthroat market.

• **Networking and Relationship Building**:

Building and leveraging a strong network is a key quality of successful entrepreneurs. Whether it's framing associations, looking for mentorship, or interfacing with industry peers, they perceive the worth of connections. Arranging gives critical pieces of information, backing, and astounding entryways that add to the advancement of their undertakings.

• **Continuous Learning Mindset:**

The business scene is constantly creating, and productive business visionaries embrace a mindset of relentless learning. They stay inquisitive, search out new information, and adjust to arising patterns. This obligation to learning keeps them educated as well as positions them as trend-setters in their particular businesses.

Generally, the excursion to pioneering achievement is as much about private characteristics for what it's worth about business discernment.These key qualities structure the DNA of thriving money managers, framing their system, decisions, and at last, the advancement of their undertakings.

Chapter 1: Finding Your Business Idea

In this part, we set out on the instigative excursion of finding your optimal business thought. Whether you are a seasoned professional exploring new gambles or a complete neophyte eager to dive into entrepreneurship, finding the right business conception is a pivotal first step.

• Unleash Your Passion

Your business idea should be a reflection of what you love and are authentically passionate about.Think about your interests, interests, and the impacts that cause you to forget about time. Releasing your energy guarantees a satisfying excursion as well as lays the root for supported loyalty.

• Identify Market Needs

Look around; every gap is an implicit occasion. Successful business ideas frequently stem from addressing existing requirements or solving problems. Pay attention to the pain points people experience in their diurnal lives or identify areas where existing results fall suddenly. Your business thought transforms into a significant result to these hardships.

• Solve Your Own Problem

occasionally, the stylish ideas come from particular gests . Ponder hardships you've faced or issues you've encountered.Chances are, if it affected you, others might be grappling with the same issues. Crafting a result to your own problem can lead to a business idea that resonates with a broader followership.

• Explore Trends and Emerging Markets

Stay in tune with current trends and emerging requests. diligence evolves, and new openings arise with changing consumer preferences and technological advancements. Your coming big idea might be hidden in an emerging trend or an untapped request waiting to be explored.

• influence Your Chops and moxie

Your unique chops and moxie form a treasure trove for implicit business ideas. Consider what you excel at — whether it's a professional skill, a hobbyhorse you've mastered, or a unique gift. Turning your chops into a business can provide a strong foundation built on what you formerly knew and love.

• Conduct Market Research

Investigate the request geography to understand existing businesses, consumer demands, and challengers. Conduct checks, interviews, or utilize online tools to gather perceptivity. request exploration not only validates your idea but also attendants you in shaping it to meet the specific requirements of your target followership.

• Collaborate and Brainstorm

Two heads are frequently better than one. Engage in cooperative brainstorming sessions with peers, mentors, or friends. Alternate points of view can start novel thoughts or refine existing ones. A cooperative conceptualizing approach can uncover bits of knowledge and points you could have neglected.

• Test and Validate

Before completely committing to your idea, test and validate it. Create a prototype, conduct a small- scale launch, or gather feedback from implicit customers. Validation is a pivotal step in ensuring that your business idea isn't only doable but also resonates with your intended audience.

• Seek Inspiration from Success Stories

Draw inspiration from successful entrepreneurs and their journeys. Gaining from their encounters can give experiences and move innovative reasoning. While their paths may not be replicable, success stories frequently share common elements, similar as resilience, adaptability, and a keen understanding of the market.

• Embrace Iteration and Evolution

Your original idea is just the starting point. Embrace the course of cycle and development. Be open to refining your concept based on feedback, request changes, or particular growth. Successful businesses frequently undergo transformations as they adapt to the dynamic nature of entrepreneurship.

Remember, finding your business idea is a dynamic and particular journey. It's tied in with consolidating your energy with market amazing open doors, distinguishing issues worth settling, and remaining open to motivation from beautiful sources. Your entrepreneurial spark awaits, and the journey of discovery begins with that first idea.

Identifying personal interests and skills

In starting your business, understanding yourself is the compass guiding your way. Here's a sneak peek into identifying your personal interests and skills

•Tap into Your Passions:

Take a moment to wander through what truly lights a fire in your heart. This is worrying about diving into your enthusiasm and sorting out what exercises truly impact you.

•Spotting Patterns in Pleasure:

There's a rhythm to the things you love. Finding those examples assists with describing your one of a kind mix of capacities and interest.

• Releasing Interest:

Follow the path of interest. This is your opportunity to find new interests and dive into what drives you.

• Outside Opinions Matter:

Sometimes, others see things we might miss. Search for input from loved ones, associates, and allies to gain new perspectives on your tendencies and strong regions.

•Your Skills: Your Toolkit:

Dive into your skills toolkit—both the technical know-how and those softer skills. Find the abilities that set the foundation for your pioneering tries.

•Reflecting on Your Wins:

Take a stroll down the achievement lane. What achievements do you feel pleased with? Contemplating what you've accomplished could help you in finding the cutoff points and redirection rehearses that present to you an energy of satisfaction.

•Embrace the New:

Ever thought of trying something completely different? This is the signal to welcome uncertainty. Investigate your secret capacities and drives by accepting an open door at new pursuits.

• Work Wisdom:

Your job journey holds nuggets of insight. Take into account the input from your work experiences to identify the elements that truly align with your skills and interests.

•Connecting the Dots:

It's where the magic happens—the sweet spot where what fires you up aligns with what you're naturally good at.

Market research for potential opportunities

Statistical surveying is the main piece of beginning a business since it gives you valuable data about potential open doors that can assist you with pursuing vital choices. A full technique for statistical surveying concentrates on that gander at many sides of the business world.

•Figuring out the Main interest group:

A thorough understanding of your target audience is essential to starting a successful business journey. Learn about people's inclinations, affinities, and economics.The development of a product or service that will appeal to customers and the identification of their needs require this information.

•Industry and Contender Investigation:

To identify prevailing trends, technological advancements, and potential disruptors, examine the industry landscape as a whole. Look at contenders all the while to find out about their techniques, assets, and shortcomings.By looking at changed choices, you can find unfilled requirements in the market that your organization can fill.

•Information Assortment Strategies:

Send a blend of quantitative and subjective exploration strategies. Overviews, interviews, center gatherings, and observational investigations give different viewpoints. Influence online overviews and examination apparatuses to assemble quantitative information, supplemented by subjective bits of knowledge from direct cooperations with expected clients and industry specialists.

•Shopper Conduct and Buying Examples:

Understanding buyer conduct is integral to anticipating buying designs. Research factors affecting purchasing choices, as mental triggers, brand responsibility, and the effect of displaying channels.Perceiving these examples permits you to tailor your contributions and advertising systems likewise.

•Market Interest and Evaluating Procedures:

Analyze the level of interest in your product or service in the identified target market. Utilize methods like interest gauging to expect future patterns. All the while, lay out a hearty evaluating technique by considering creation costs, contender estimating, and saw worth to the client.

•Innovative and Administrative Contemplations:

Keep up with developments in technology that could affect your industry. Additionally, explore the administrative scene to guarantee consistency with regulations and guidelines. Being proactive in adjusting to mechanical moves and understanding administrative systems defends your business against unexpected difficulties.

• Making use of industry reports and online tools:

Influence the force of online apparatuses and stages to assemble continuous information. Screen virtual entertainment for patterns and client feelings. For exhaustive data on macroeconomic factors, market size, and advancement projections, counsel market studies and industry reports.

•Joint effort and Mentorship:

Tap into the abundance of information inside your industry by working together with specialists or looking for mentorship. Drawing in with experienced experts gives basic viewpoints and can assist you with staying away from ordinary entanglements.Organizing inside your industry encourages associations that might prompt unexpected open doors.

•Specialties and Arising Patterns:

Examine the market for emerging trends and untapped niches. Distinguish regions where current arrangements miss the mark and improve to satisfy idle needs. Adjusting to developing patterns positions your business at the bleeding edge of progress, improving its drawn out manageability.

A robust market research strategy is not a one-time effort but an ongoing process. Regularly revisit and update your analyses to stay abreast of dynamic market conditions. You can pursue all around informed choices, diminish dangers, and make the most of the various open doors introduced by the business scene with the data obtained from extensive statistical surveying.

Chapter 2: Creating a Solid Business Plan

Give a quick overview of your business model and some important financial projections..This far reaching record fills in as a guide, framing your business objectives, systems, and the way to benefit. The following are important considerations:

• Leader Outline:

Start with a succinct outline of your business. Feature your central goal, vision, and the issue your item or administration addresses. Give a fast outline of your plan of action and a few significant monetary projections.

• Description of the company:

Investigate your company's specifics, including its location, history, and legal structure. Make sense of your extraordinary incentive and what separates your business on the lookout.

• Market Examination:

Show that you know a lot about your industry and your target audience. Present the consequences of your statistical surveying, including a far reaching examination of your potential client base and contender investigations. Distinguish market difficulties and amazing open doors.

• Management and organization:

Describe the organization's structure, including the roles played by key team members. Feature the abilities and skills that each colleague offers of real value. Your confidence in your ability to carry out the business plan is bolstered by this section.

• Item or Administration Offering:

Give point by point data about your item or administration. Sort out its parts, benefits, and the issue it handles for clients. If pertinent, examine the advancement cycle and any licensed innovation contemplations.

• Advertising and Deals Methodology:

Detail your arrangement for coming to and gaining clients. Characterize your interest group, frame advertising channels, and clarify your deals procedure. Incorporate a financial plan for showcasing drives and deals projections.

• Subsidizing Solicitation (if relevant):

If you want to get money from outside sources, be specific about how much money you need, what you want it for, and how you will use it. Depict what is going on exhaustively, including any advances or speculations you have.

• **Monetary Projections:**

Include income statements, balance sheets, and cash flow statements in your comprehensive financial forecasts. Use down to earth doubts considering your factual looking over and industry designs.Financial backers and partners will intently investigate this segment.

• **Risk Assessment:**

Recognize expected dangers and difficulties your business might confront. Reveal your ability to adjust to changing circumstances by examining strategies for diminishing these risks. A cautious gamble examination exhibits a proactive and reasonable methodology.

• **Execution Plan:**

Give a clarification of how you will watch out and assess your organization's presentation. Incorporate courses of events, achievements, and obligations. A very organized execution plan guarantees a smooth execution of your techniques.

• Observation and Assessment:

Set benchmarks and key execution pointers (KPIs). Check your arrangement consistently and make changes in view of genuine outcomes and changes on the lookout.

• Appendices:

Give specific instructions on how to put your business plan into action, detailed data from market research, or additional financial information should all be included. The business plan's appendices provide evidence to back up claims made in the main body.

A fruitful marketable strategy should have a reasonable vision for the future, cautious exploration, and tender loving care. Reliably return to and update your game plan as your business creates, promising it remains a strong instrument that coordinates your flourishing.

Importance of a business plan

A business plan for entrepreneurs is like a roadmap for their dreams. It lays out what the business wants to achieve and spills the beans on how it's going to get there – you know, the wholesaler, marketing, and making cool products part. It resembles the fight plan for transforming thoughts into the real world!

It might frame every individual objective for the business, including where finances will come from, how workers will add to the objectives and how the business can benefit.

Beginning a business can be productive while likewise being perilous. You can decide the means you really want to take and the business' arranged objectives by making a business plan ahead of time. At the point when you make a reliable methodology, this is your opportunity to contemplate your business thought's necessities and possible results. An appealing philosophy can help you with pinpointing unmistakable targets and obligations.

A field-tested strategy is significant for organizations for different reasons. A few of these reasons include:

•It sets up an arrangement while beginning another business

A lot goes into starting a new business. As well as concocting a business thought, you likewise need to cement the particulars of the business, similar to what administrations or items you will sell, where you will carry on with work and who will work for the organization. A marketable strategy can assist with giving direction in this cycle, which can likewise assist with keeping away from botches en route. It can offer you a comprehension into the means you truly need to take to begin your business, as well as the resources you ought to get.

•To conduct the necessary research

You might create a business plan before even deciding to open a business.Composing a strategy expects that you direct the important exploration, which can be useful in choosing if beginning a business checks out. You could likewise make a strategy on the off chance that you mean to steer your current business toward another path. By working out the subtleties and funds of the new arrangement, you can decide whether a shift will be productive. This incorporates characterizing your market, pinpointing who your clients are and the way that you will contact them.

•To evaluate competitors and find your audience

Another piece of making a field-tried procedure is investigating the continuous associations in the business where you want to work.. You can better anticipate how you will reach customers by determining where your rivals do not currently reach them. It can likewise assist you with picking your main interest group.

•Sets objectives for employees and managers

Setting and estimating goals will guarantee that representatives and directors are sure about their obligations. By laying out clear objectives and assumptions, this can likewise help you in choosing the best representatives for your business.business plan sets the expectations of the business from the beginning. In the event that you change or update your objectives, a field-tested strategy can assist with sharing these new goals, giving construction and responsibility.

•Sets goals for you as an entrepreneur

Laying out clear objectives is likewise useful for you as a business person. You can utilize a marketable strategy to list explicit objectives that you need to accomplish, alongside deadlines. As a business person, you can involve this as a manual for sorting out your everyday obligations and consider yourself responsible.

•To determine when new employees are needed

You'll require more workers to assist you with everyday undertakings as your business develops and your income rises.However, recruiting individuals before you're prepared to extend can lessen your benefits. A strategy can assist you with assessing the ideal opportunity to welcome extra staff. It can likewise aid plainly characterizing each position's liabilities and assumptions. You can likewise utilize your arrangement to figure out what abilities to search for while recruiting.

•Assists you in making important business decisions

Decision-making is an important task as an entrepreneur. A few choices, similar to when to lease another space or extend the business, are not generally simple to make. With a reasonable strategy set up, you can decide the particular times or objectives you should meet to pursue these significant choices.

•To know when to sell your business

You may choose to sell your business and move onto different thoughts. Deciding when to sell can be a difficult decision. You can set a course of events and decide when it is the perfect opportunity to sell your business by obviously characterizing your goals and wanted results. The data in your strategy can likewise be helpful while selling the business since it framcs the objectives and achievements of the organization and can expand its worth.

•To determine how you will find funding

You might choose to take out a business credit or welcome financial backers to be a piece of your business. New organizations frequently require reserves and a marketable strategy can assist you with introducing your plans to likely financial backers. On the off chance that you apply for a business credit, you might require an intensive marketable strategy to show your business thoughts to the bank moneylender as well. A business plan can also aid you decide how much money you will need to start, and operate, your business.

•To understand when/how you will profit

Salary is not always clear as an entrepreneur. However, a business plan is necessary if you want to estimate when investors can anticipate a return on investment or how long it will take you to make money. A strategy records the normal expenses of the business, as well as the income.You can anticipate when and how your business will turn a profit as long as you accomplish the financial objectives outlined in the plan.

•Help you predict problems

A field-tested strategy can likewise assist you with foreseeing expected issues, as sluggish seasons or changing client patterns or propensities. You might have the option to get ready and beat these difficulties early on with a marketable strategy.

•Provides a valuation for the business

Putting esteem on an independent venture can be troublesome, however it is here and there important. Whether you need to remember it for your home, show it available to be purchased or you really want an incentive for charges, a marketable strategy can be a significant asset. Giving your field-tested strategy to a bookkeeper can likewise assist them with working out an exact incentive for your business.

•To share your marketable strategies with colleagues and family

When you start a business, former coworkers and family members will probably ask a lot of questions about what you do. You can answer these sales by drafting a dependable methodology and figuring out your targets and plans for them.

•To provide you with guidance during difficult situations

As a financial specialist, you could have to oversee things like laborer battles or even genuine difficulties. An unmistakable strategy can assist you with managing these issues, recognizing the reason for your business and what you desire to accomplish.

•To create an effective marketing strategy

Once you have a business, you will need to reach customers through marketing. Setting clear objectives for the business can assist you with pinpointing who your clients are, yet in addition the most effective way to contact them. This can also aid you with boosting your promoting spending plan and increment your revenue.

•To allow you the best opportunity of accomplishment

The objective of a business venture is to claim a fruitful business. While no business thought is ensured, having a reasonable marketable strategy set up builds your odds of coming out on top. Getting back to the marketable strategy occasionally can likewise assist with helping you to remember why you turned into a business visionary and can assist you with pulling together on the mission statement of the business.

•Manage cash flow for the business

You'll need to decide how to spend your profits once they start coming in. You might utilize benefits to take compensation, reinvest in the business or track down new items or administrations to sell. This can be made simpler by including your cash flow plans in your business plan.

•To determine the success of the business

Clear set of objectives in a business plan can help you measure success. Counting key execution pointers licenses you to know how to evaluate your headway toward your goals. This data can be used to figure out what parts of the association are getting along honorably and which ought to be gotten to a higher level. You can in like manner use it to choose if you truly need new plans or goals.

Step-by-step guide to developing a business plan

• Write an executive summary

This is the first page of your business plan. Consider it your brief presentation. It ought to incorporate a statement of purpose, a concise portrayal of the items or administrations offered, and a wide rundown of your monetary development plans.

However the leader outline is the main thing your financial backers will pursue, it may very well be simpler to compose it last. Like that, you can feature data you've recognized while composing different areas that carefully describe the situation.

• Describe your company

Next up is your company description, which should contain information like:

Your business's registered name.

Address of your business location.

The names of significant individuals in the business . Make a point to feature interesting abilities or specialized mastery among colleagues.

In addition, your business structure, such as a sole proprietorship, partnership, or corporation, should be described in your company description, along with the percentage of ownership each owner holds and their involvement in the business.

Last but not least, it ought to talk about your business's past and present. The reader will be better able to comprehend your objectives in the following section as a result of this.

• **State your business goals**

The third part of a business plan is an objective statement.This segment illuminates precisely the exact thing you might want to achieve, both in the close to term and over the long haul.

You can utilize this part to make sense of why you have a reasonable requirement for the assets, how the funding will assist your business with developing, and how you intend to accomplish your development objectives in the event that you are searching for a business credit or an external speculation. The key is to give a reasonable clarification of the open door introduced and how the credit or speculation will develop your organization.

For instance, in the event that your business is sending off a subsequent product offering, you could make sense of how the credit will assist your organization with sending off the new item and the amount you figure deals will increment throughout the following three years thus.

• Portray your things and organizations

In this part, cautiously depict the things or organizations you propose or want to offer.

The following ought to be included:

- A clarification of how your item or administration functions.

- The pricing model for your product or service.

- The typical customers you serve.

- Your approach to order fulfillment and supply chain

- Your sales strategy.

- Your distribution strategy.

You can also talk about your product's or service's trademarks and patents, either already in use or pending.

• Do your market research

Loan specialists and financial backers will need to understand what separates your item from your opposition. Define your rivals in the section of your market analysis. Talk about what they get along nicely and what you could develop. Please explain if you are catering to a different or underserved market.

• list your plan for marketing and sales.

Here, you can discuss how you intend to get individuals to purchase your items or administrations or how you intend to fabricate client reliability that will inspire them to purchase from you in the future.

• Perform a business financial analysis

If you are a startup, you may not have much information on your business finances yet. Nonetheless, assuming that you're a current business, you'll need to incorporate an income or profit-and-loss statement, a balance sheet that rundowns your assets and liabilities, and a cash flow statement that shows how money comes into and leaves the organization.

You may also include criteria similar as Net profit margin, the percentage of revenue you keep as net income. Current ratio is the measurement of your liquidity and capability to repay debts. Accounts delinquent turnover ratio a measurement of how constantly you collect on receivables per time. Still, there's a fantastic spot to put charts and graphs, If you want individualities reading your plan to understand your company's fiscal health more.

• Make fiscal projections

This is a critical part of your business plan if you 're seeking backing or investors. It makes sense of how your organization will make sufficient pay to repay the credit or how financial backers will take care of you. Then, you 'll give your business's yearly or daily sales, expenses and profit estimates over at least a three- time period — with the unborn figures assuming you 've obtained a new loan. Precisely examine your former fiscal statements because delicacy is essential before making projections. Your objectives might be forceful, still they ought to likewise bc sensible.

• Add fresh information to an appendix

List any supporting information or fresh accouterments that you could n't fit in away, similar as resumes of crucial workers, licenses, equipment leases, permits, patents, bills, bank statements, contracts and particular and business credit history.However, you may consider adding a table of contents at the beginning of this section, If the appendix is long.

Chapter 3: Legal Considerations and Structure

The following should be considered:

• **Legal Structure:**

Clearly define the legal structure of your business (e.g., sole proprietorship, partnership, LLC, corporation).

clarify why you picked the structure you did, taking into account factors like responsibility, taxation, and managerial simplicity.

• **Business Registration:**

Outline the steps taken or planned for registering your business with the appropriate authorities.

Check that local, state, and federal business registration rules are followed.

• Licenses and Permits:

List any licenses and permits required for your industry and location.

Detail the process undertaken to secure these licenses and your plan for ongoing compliance.

• Protection of Intellectual Property:

Recognize and portray any protected innovation related to your business (e.g., brand names, licenses, copyrights).

Outline steps taken to protect and register intellectual property if applicable.

• Agreements and Arrangements:

Give an outline of key agreements and arrangements applicable to your business tasks.

Highlight any legal partnerships, client agreements, or vendor contracts and their terms.

• Employment Laws:

Familiarize yourself with and adhere to employment laws relevant to your location.

Clearly define employment relationships, contracts, and employee rights.

• Data Privacy and Security:

Address how your business will handle customer and employee data.

Evaluate the relevant data protection requirements that are being followed and that data privacy policies are being implemented.

• Environmental Regulations:

Identify and comply with any environmental regulations pertinent to your industry.

Outline measures taken to minimize the environmental impact of your business operations.

• **Taxation:**

Know about and follow the rules for local, state, and federal taxes..

Clearly define your business's tax structure and how taxes will be managed and reported.

• **Observance of health and wellness regulations:**

Implement health and safety protocols in accordance with relevant regulations.

Outline measures taken to ensure a safe working environment for employees and customers.

• **Business Insurance:**

Detail the types of insurance coverage your business carries (e.g., liability, property, workers' compensation).

Check that your insurance coverage corresponds to the unique hazards of your sector.

• Exit Strategy:

Consider and outline an exit strategy in case of unforeseen circumstances.

Define procedures for business dissolution, sale, or transfer of ownership, if applicable.

• Ongoing Compliance:

Develop a plan for ongoing legal compliance and monitoring.
Regularly review and update your legal considerations to adapt to changes in regulations or business circumstances.

Taking care of these lawful contemplations and characterizing a strong corporate design are basic for building a strong legitimate establishment. Associate with real specialists to ensure total consistency and security for your business.

Choosing the right legal structure for your business

Business people should settle on an urgent conclusion about their lawful design since it influences everything from risk to tax collection. Here is a bit by bit manual for assist you with exploring this pivotal decision:

• Examine Your Business Objectives:

Clarify your short-term and long-term business objectives.
Understand whether you prefer a simple structure or foresee potential scalability.

• Understand Different Legal Structures:

Research common legal structures, including sole proprietorship, partnership, LLC, and corporation.

Consider factors like obligation, tax collection, the board adaptability, and simplicity of development.

• Evaluate Personal Liability:

Assess the level of personal liability protection needed.
Understand how each legal structure shields personal assets from business debts and legal actions.

• Tax Implications:

Inspect the expense ramifications of each legitimate construction.
Consider your solace with individual and business charge commitments, and investigate choices for limiting assessment risk.

• Management Structure:

Evaluate how you want to manage and make decisions within your business.

Differentiate between structures that allow for sole decision-making and those requiring input from partners or a board of directors.

• Consider Complexity and Formalities:

Determine your comfort level with administrative tasks and paperwork.
Comprehend the customs related with each legitimate design, like yearly gatherings and announcing necessities.

• Flexibility for Ownership Changes:

Consider the ease with which ownership can be transferred or new owners can be added.
Evaluate the flexibility of each structure in accommodating changes in ownership over time.

• Cost of Formation and Maintenance:

Assess the initial costs of forming each legal structure.

Consider continuous upkeep costs, like charges and authoritative costs.

•   Industry   and   Financial   backer Assumptions:

Investigate the legal structures that are generally accepted in your sector.
Learn about the preferences of potential investors because some structures might appeal to them more.

• Seek the assistance of a Financial and Legal Expert:

Consult with legal and financial professionals to get personalized advice.

Examine the particular necessities and subtleties of your business to pursue an educated decision.

• **Think about Future Development:**

Anticipate the growth trajectory of your business.

Choose a legal structure that accommodates expansion and potential changes in business dynamics.

Review and Rethink Occasionally:

Regularly review your business structure in light of changing circumstances.

Be available to re-evaluating and change your lawful design to line up with the developing requirements of your business.

Picking the right legitimate construction is an urgent starting point for your business. Ensure that the construction you pick is viable with your organization's targets and mitigates possible dangers by leading careful examination and looking for proficient guidance.

Registering your business and compliance essentials

Your company must be established through a series of actions, with registration and compliance playing a crucial role. Here's a comprehensive guide to help you ensure a smooth process:

• Choose a Business Name:

Select a unique and memorable business name that aligns with your brand.
Check the availability of the chosen name and ensure it complies with local naming regulations.

• Determine Your Legal Structure:

Choose the legal structure that best suits your business, considering factors like liability, taxation, and management flexibility.

Register your business as a sole proprietorship, partnership, LLC, corporation, or any other suitable structure.

• Get a Government Business ID Number (EIN):

If your business has employees or operates as a corporation or partnership, obtain an EIN from the IRS.
This unique identifier is essential for tax purposes and opening a business bank account.

• Register with the Relevant Authorities:

Complete the necessary registration processes with local, state, and federal authorities.
This may include registering with state business offices, obtaining licenses, and complying with industry-specific regulations.

• Acquire Necessary Business Licenses and Permits:

Distinguish the licenses and allowances for your particular industry and area.
Ensure compliance with local, state, and federal regulations, and renew licenses as needed.

• Open a Business Bank Account:

•Separate your business funds from individual budgets by starting a committed business financial balance.
•Provide the bank with your EIN and other required documentation.

• Set Up an Accounting System:

Implement an accounting system to track income, expenses, and other financial transactions.
 Accurate record keeping and compliance with tax regulations will be made easier by this system.

• Understand Employment Laws:

Familiarize yourself with employment laws which are relevant to your business, including minimum wage, working hours, and employee rights.
Clearly define employment relationships and comply with labor regulations.

• Comply with Tax Obligations:

Figure out your duty commitments at the nearby, state, and government levels.
Keep accurate financial records, file tax returns on time, and make necessary tax payments.

• Implementation of Data Privacy Policies:

Establish data privacy policies if your business handles customer or employee data.
Ensure compliance with data protection regulations and safeguard sensitive information.

• Keep up with changes to regulations:

Regularly monitor changes in regulations that may affect your business.
Get customary updates about charge regulations, authorizing prerequisites, and industry-explicit guidelines.

• Get Business Protection:

Survey the particular dangers related to your business and get proper protection and inclusion. This may include general liability insurance, property insurance, and other forms of coverage based on your industry.

• Go through Normal Consistency Reviews:

Periodically review your business operations to ensure ongoing compliance.
Conduct internal audits to find and fix any potential problems with compliance.

• Get Professional Advice :

Consult with legal and financial professionals to navigate complex compliance requirements.
Obtain guidance on industry-specific regulations and legal obligations.

Diligently following these steps and staying attuned to compliance essentials, you establish a solid foundation for your business. Regularly review and update your compliance practices to adapt to changes in regulations and ensure the sustained success of your venture.

Chapter 4: Financing Your Venture

Sending off and growing a business frequently requires capital, and understanding how to fund your endeavor is urgent.Here's a comprehensive guide to help you navigate the intricacies of securing funds:

• Assess Your Funding Needs:

Startup Costs: Determine the initial expenses required to launch your business, including equipment, licenses, and marketing.

Working Capital: Calculate ongoing operational expenses such as rent, utilities, and salaries.

• Explore Personal Savings:

Consider using personal savings as an initial source of capital.

Assess the level of risk you're comfortable taking with your own funds.

• Family and Friends:

Seek financial support from family and friends who believe in your venture.

Obviously convey terms and assumptions to stay away from false impressions..

• Angel Investors:

Explore angel investors who provide capital in exchange for equity.

Set up a convincing field-tested strategy to draw in heavenly messenger speculation.

• Venture Capital:

For high-growth potential businesses, consider venture capital.

Be ready for a significant equity stake and rigorous due diligence.

• Small Business Loans:

Investigate loans from banks or financial institutions.

Explore Small Business Administration (SBA) loans for favorable terms and lower interest rates.

• Crowdfunding:

Utilize crowdfunding platforms to raise funds from a large number of people.

Lay out a convincing effort that plainly characterizes compensations for buyers.

• Grants and Competitions:

Look for grants from government agencies, nonprofits, or industry-specific organizations. Engage in business competitions offering cash prizes and networking opportunities.

• Strategic Partnerships:

Explore partnerships with larger companies that can provide financial support.

Ensure alignment of goals and expectations in the partnership.

• Bootstrapping:

Take a bootstrapping technique by minimizing expenses and zeroing in on regular turns of events.

Reinvest benefits once more into the business for feasible extension.

• Elective Financing Alternatives:

Investigate elective subsidizing decisions like receipt supporting, ascertaining, or equipment leasing.

Analyze each choice's terms and repercussions.

• Create a comprehensive financial arrangement:

Encourage a comprehensive financial plan that demonstrates income projections, costs, and income.

Clearly state how the money will be used to achieve business objectives.

• Demonstrate Traction:

Share concrete proof of market engagement with potential financial partners.

Give data on how to get new customers.

Understanding startup costs

Startup costs are the costs caused during the strategy associated with making another business. All associations are remarkable, so they require different sorts of startup costs. Online organizations have unexpected necessities in comparison to block and-mortars;

bistros have unexpected prerequisites in comparison to book shops. Be that as it may, a couple of costs are normal to most business types.

• The Marketable strategy

Fundamental for the startup exertion is making a field-tested strategy — a point by point guide of the new business. A marketable strategy powers thought of the different startup costs. Misjudging costs erroneously increments expected net benefit, a circumstance that bodes well for no entrepreneur.

Research Costs

Cautious examination of the business and purchaser cosmetics should be directed prior to beginning a business. To help them in the assessment cycle, some entrepreneurs would prefer to employ statistical surveying organizations.

For entrepreneurs who decide to follow this course, the cost of recruiting these specialists should be remembered for the strategy.

Acquiring Expenses

Firing up any sort of business requires an imbuement of capital. A business can obtain capital in two ways: support by means of obligation and value. As a rule, value funding involves the issuance of stock, yet this doesn't have any significant bearing to most independent ventures, which are ownerships.

Obligation as an independent venture credit is the most probable wellspring of funding for proprietors of private companies. Entrepreneurs can frequently get credits from banks, reserve funds establishments, etc.

Protection, Permit, and License Expenses

Numerous organizations are supposed to submit to wellbeing assessments and approvals to acquire specific permits to operate and allow. A few organizations could require fundamental licenses while others need industry-explicit grants.

Conveying protection to cover your workers, clients, business resources, and yourself can assist with shielding your own resources from any liabilities that might emerge.

Innovative Costs

Innovative costs incorporate the expense of a site, data frameworks, and programming, including bookkeeping and retail location (POS) programming, for a business. A few business people choose to re-fitting these capacities to various associations to get a good deal on money and benefits.

Hardware and Supplies

Each business requires a few types of hardware and essential supplies. Prior to adding hardware costs to the rundown of startup costs, a choice must be made to rent or purchase.

The condition of your funds will have a significant effect in this choice. Regardless of whether you have sufficient means to purchase hardware, inescapable costs might make renting, with the expectation to purchase sometime in the future, a reasonable choice. Nonetheless, it is critical to recall that, no matter what the money position, a rent may not generally be ideal, contingent on the kind of gear and terms of the rent.

Publicizing and Advancement

Another organization or new company is probably not going to prevail without advancing itself. Notwithstanding, advancing a business involves significantly more than putting promotions in a nearby paper.

It likewise incorporates promoting — all that an organization does to draw in clients to the business. Showcasing has become such a science that any benefit is gainful, so outer committed promoting organizations are most frequently recruited.

Worker Costs

Organizations intending to enlist representatives should make arrangements for wages, pay rates, and advantages, otherwise called the expense of work.

Inability to repay representatives satisfactorily can end in low resolve, rebellion, and terrible exposure, which can all be sad to an organization.

Extra Startup Cost Contemplations

Have some additional cash put away for any neglected or surprising costs. Most organizations come up short since they miss the mark on money to manage unforeseen issues during the business season.

It is essential to take note of the fact that the startup costs for a sole ownership vary from the startup costs for an organization or enterprise. A few extra costs an organization could cause incorporate the legitimate expense of drafting an association understanding and state enlistment charges.

Different costs that might apply more to an organization incorporate charges for recording articles of consolidation, standing rules, and terms of unique stock testaments.

Sending off another business can empower. In any case, becoming involved with the energy and dismissing the subtleties can prompt disappointment. Above whatever else, notice and talk with other people who have voyaged this street previously — no one can really tell where you could gain proficiency with the business counsel that assists your specific business with succeeding.

Exploring funding options, including loans and investors

Setting up a business frequently includes somewhat more money than a stash can deal with. Dread not, valiant business people, for this part outfits you with the information to explore the subsidizing oceans, from bank credits to private backers and then some.

Credit Language:

Bank Advances: These are your reliable choices, such as getting from your nearby bank or credit association. They offer security and faithfulness, yet go with advanced costs and serious guaranteeing processes.Be ready to pitch your strategy and financials like a genius!

SBA Advances:

The Independent company Organization (SBA) is your administration companion, offering credits with lower financing costs and more adaptable terms for qualifying organizations. Consider them the predatory lenders with an endearing personality.

Credit extensions:

Envision an enchanted Visa for your business. These lines give consistent admittance to cash, making them ideal for covering surprising costs or intermittent variances. Simply overspended, can transform wizardry into a monetary bad dream.

Financial backer Intel:

Holy messengers: Consider holy messengers big-hearted mythical beasts monitoring a gold mine of money. They're well off people who put resources into promising new companies, frequently in return for value or a seat at the board table.Be ready to be astonished by your energy, potential, and market data.

Financial speculators (VCs): These are the sharks of the venture world, orbiting new businesses with high development potential. They contribute gobs of cash, however anticipate enormous returns and a quick leave technique. On the off chance that your business is a rocket transport, VCs are the fuel.

Crowdfunding:

This web-based stage is like a computerized heat deal for your business thoughts. You pitch your venture to the majority, and assuming that enough individuals purchase in (in a real sense), you get financed. It's an incredible method for testing market interest and fabricating local areas, yet be ready for the promoting hustle.

Keep in mind,

Matchmaking Matters: Pick the subsidizing choice that lines up with your business stage, needs, and hazard resistance. A credit may be the protected house, while private supporters could be your platform to the moon.

Numbers Talk: Set up a strong strategy and monetary projections. Financial backers and moneylenders need to see you've gotten your work done, not simply thrown the dice.

Try not to Be Modest: Organization, pitch, and rehash! The more individuals are familiar with your business, the more certain you are to draw in the right financing.

Chapter 5: Building a Strong Brand

Building serious areas of strength for a will be an imperative and dynamic cooperation that incorporates deliberate exercises to shape perceptions and make getting through relationships with your group. Here is an exhaustive manual for assist you with building a vigorous brand:

• Characterize Your Image System:

Obviously lucid your image's main goal, values, and remarkable selling suggestions. A strong groundwork directs all marking endeavors.

• Understand Your Listeners' perspective:

Figure out your interest group - their necessities, inclinations, and ways of behaving.

Tailor your image message and contributions to impact them.

• Make a Particular Visual Character:

Foster a critical and conspicuous logo, picking tones and text styles that mirror your image character. Consistency in visual components improves brand review.

• Reliable Marking Across Touchpoints:

Guarantee consistency in marking across all stages - from your site and online entertainment to bundling and advertising materials. Consistency assembles trust and extraordinary mastery.

• Fabricate a Convincing Brand Story:

Make a story that imparts the substance of your image. Share your excursion, values, and the effect you mean to make. A persuading story makes significant affiliations.

• Convey Extraordinary Worth:

Give top notch items or administrations that line up with your image guarantee. Reliably surpass client assumptions to fabricate trust and dedication.

• Client Driven Approach:

Put your clients at the focal point of your image technique. Pay attention to their input, address concerns quickly, and make customized encounters.

• Separate from Contenders:

Recognize what makes your image extraordinary. Feature these differentiators in your promotion to hang out in a jam-packed market.

• Construct Brand Authority:

Position yourself as a specialist in your industry.
Share huge snippets of data, participate in thought power, and add to basic discussions.

• Effectively Utilizing On the web Entertainment:

Influence online entertainment stages to draw in with your crowd. Be genuine, share your image story, and effectively partake in discussions.

• Put resources into a Successful Plan:

Put resources into a proficient plan for every visual component. A cleaned and firm plan improves believability and impressive skill.

• Worker Brand Promotion:

- Your workers are envoys of your image. Cultivate a positive work culture, and urge representatives to be advocates for your image both on the web and disconnected.

• Local area Commitment:

Effectively take part in local area occasions and drives. Building major areas of strength frequently includes contributing emphatically to the local area you serve.

• Screen and Adjust:

Consistently survey the adequacy of your image system. Remain lithe and adjust to advertise changes and advancing client inclinations.

• **Measure Brand Execution:**

Lay out key execution markers (KPIs) to gauge the progress of your marking endeavors. Examine information to comprehend what is working and where changes are required.

Creating areas of mettle is a predictable exertion that requires liability and adaptability. By reliably conveying esteem, remaining consistent with your image guarantee, and adjusting to transforms, you can make a brand that reverberates and perseveres.

Importance of branding

Branding is not just about logos and colors; it's the soul of your business. Here's why it stands at the core of success:

• First Impressions Count:

Your brand is the first handshake with your audience. It establishes a major first connection with clients and decides if they choose to investigate what you bring to the table.

• Distinct Identity:

Branding gives your business a distinctive identity. In a packed market, your character makes you stick out and assists clients with recalling that you.

• Trust Building:

A strong brand builds trust. Customers are more likely to select your products or services if your messaging and presentation are consistent.

• Customer Loyalty:

Brands that resonate emotionally create loyal customers. At the point when clients interface with your image on a more profound level, they are bound to stay faithful and become advocates.

• Competitive Edge:

In a world of choices, branding provides a competitive edge. Customers are more likely to choose you over your rivals if your brand is clearly defined and memorable.

• Value Perception:

Solid marking improves the apparent worth of your items or administrations. A brand that they trust and believe in often attracts higher prices from customers.

• Consistency Across Platforms:

Whether online, offline, or in-store, consistent branding creates a seamless experience. consistency fosters your image message and strengthens its effect.

• Communication Tool:

Your brand communicates without words. Your image recounts a story, conveying your focal objective, values, and the commitment you make to clients. Viable marking is a strong type of correspondence.

• Facilitating Expansion:

As your business grows, so does your brand. A well-established brand makes expansion into new markets or the introduction of new products smoother, as customers already recognize and trust your name.

• Emotional Connection:

Brands are more than just about products; they are about sentiments. A brand that interfaces sincerely turns into a piece of clients' lives, cultivating a relationship past exchanges.

• Long-Term Investment:

Branding is a long-term investment. A strong brand withstands challenges and stand the test of time, providing stability and resilience despite fluctuations in sales.

• Attraction of Talent:

Beyond customers, strong branding attracts talent. Workers need to be related with a brand they trust in, making enlistment and upkeep more direct for your business.

• Brand Credibility:

A well-established brand enhances your business credibility. When customers perceive a brand, they are more likely to place trust in the quality of the contributions made by that brand.

• Flexibility and Adaptability:

A strong brand provides a flexible framework for business evolution. It can adjust to changing economic situations, permitting your business to turn or extend without losing its center character.

• Risk Mitigation:

Brands act as a buffer in times of crisis.A decent brand picture can assist with relieving possible harm to your business during testing circumstances, helping in recuperation and versatility.

• Marketing Efficiency:

Effective branding streamlines marketing efforts. When your brand is well-defined, your marketing strategies become more targeted and efficient, resonating with your specific audience.

• Brand Equity:

After some time, areas of strength for a collected brand value. This immaterial resource addresses the extra worth your image brings, adding to client reliability and giving an upper hand.

• International Appeal:

For businesses eyeing global markets, a strong brand transcends cultural and language barriers. It transforms into a universally applicable and embraced image that transcends socioeconomic boundaries.

• Customer Recognition and Recall:

A memorable brand facilitates customer recognition and recall. When customers easily remember your brand, they are more likely to return, reducing the cost of customer acquisition.

• Strategic Partnerships:

Other businesses are more inclined to enter partnerships with a reputable brand. A solid brand works with open doors for key joint efforts and collusions, cultivating commonly useful connections.

• Employee Morale and Pride:

Employees take pride in being associated with a well-respected brand. A solid brand cultivates a positive inward culture, lifting representative confidence levels and making a feeling of aggregate pride.

• Sustainability and Corporate Social Responsibility (CSR):

Brands with a strong sense of purpose can lead impactful sustainability and CSR initiatives. Such undertakings not just add to social and natural prosperity yet in addition upgrade the brand's picture.

• Brand Extensions:

Successful brands can easily extend their reach through new product or service offerings. Customers are more willing to try new offerings from a brand they already trust.

• Customer Advocacy:

Strong brands cultivate brand advocates. Fulfilled clients become your best advertisers, imparting their positive encounters and proposals to other people, intensifying your range.

• Embracing Digital Transformation:

In the computerized age, major areas of strength for a brand presence is fundamental. A successful advanced brand technique guarantees that your business stays pertinent and apparent in the consistently developing computerized scene.

Marking is the foundation of your business' personality and achievement. It reaches out a long way past shallow components, impacting each feature of your tasks and communications with clients and partners. Building areas of strength for an is a venture that yields long haul profits, molding the story of your business in the hearts and psyches of your customers.

Creating a compelling brand identity

Making a convincing brand character is basic for your business. Start by portraying your picture's characteristics, mission, and momentous selling centers. Make a critical and flexible logo that mirrors your image character. Consistency is key – maintain uniformity in colors, fonts, and imagery across all platforms. Foster a convincing brand story that reverberates with your ideal interest group. Participate in statistical surveying to grasp your rivals and crowd inclinations. At last, guarantee your image imparts legitimacy and assembles close to home associations with clients, encouraging trust and dedication.

Past the rudiments, lay out a durable visual personality with proficient plan components. Pick a variety range that lines up with your image's character and resounds with your interest group. Select text styles that are not difficult to peruse and mirror your image's tone.

Create a memorable tagline that encapsulates your brand message succinctly. Utilize storytelling in your marketing materials to humanize your brand and connect with customers on a personal level. Consistently apply your brand elements to all touchpoints, from your website and social media to packaging and promotional materials.

Consider the overall customer experience – every interaction should reinforce your brand identity.

Screen and adjust your marking system in light of market patterns and client criticism to remain applicable and serious. Building a persuading brand character is a constant cycle that creates with your business.

Laying out a convincing brand character is a complex cycle that includes an essential mix of innovative articulation, market understanding, and reliable correspondence. Here is a nitty gritty manual for assisting you with making a brand personality that reverberates and enraptures your main interest group.

- **Define Your Brand Foundation:**

Start by clearly defining your brand's values, mission, and vision. Recognize your exceptional selling focuses - what separates your business from rivals? Utilize these differentiators to shape your image account.

• Craft a Memorable Logo:

Your logo is a visual depiction of your picture. Work with an expert originator to make a logo that isn't just outwardly engaging yet in addition lines up with your image character.

Ensure that your logo is versatile and works well across various platforms and mediums.

• Maintain Consistency:

Consistency is a cornerstone of successful branding. Lay out a uniform variety range, typography, and symbolism across the entirety of your image materials.

Consistent branding fosters recognition and builds trust. At the point when individuals experience your image, they ought to have a durable and natural experience.

• Visual Identity:

Dive into the visual aspects of your brand. Select a color palette that matches with your target audience and reflects the emotions you want your brand to evoke.

Choose fonts that align with your brand's tone – whether it's modern and sleek or classic and traditional.

• Craft a Compelling Tagline:

Develop a tagline that succinctly communicates your brand's essence. A vital slogan can exemplify your image message and establish a long term connection.

• Tell Your Brand Story:

Engage your audience by telling a compelling brand story. Share the excursion of your image, the difficulties you've made due, and the attributes that drive your business.

Humanize your brand – people connect with stories, and a well-crafted narrative can create emotional bonds.

• Market Research:

Conduct thorough market research to understand your competitors and the preferences of your target audience. Distinguish holes in the market that your image can fill.

Stay updated on industry trends to make sure your brand remains relevant and innovative.

• Authenticity is Key:

Authenticity builds trust. Guarantee that your image informing and activities line up with your expressed qualities. Not being consistent can crumble trust and legitimacy.

- **Customer Experience:**

Consider every touchpoint as an opportunity to reinforce your brand identity. From your site and web-based entertainment presence to bundling and client support, guarantee a strong brand insight.

- **Adapt and Evolve:**

The business landscape is dynamic. Regularly assess your brand strategy, adapt to market trends, and incorporate customer feedback. A brand that evolves with the times remains relevant.

Keep in mind, making a convincing brand character is certainly not a one-time task yet a continuous cycle. Remain sensitive to your crowd, industry shifts, and your image's development direction to guarantee that your personality stays significant and thunderous.

Developing a marketing plan

Fostering a far reaching showcasing plan includes key preparation and fastidious execution.Here's a detailed guide to help you create a robust marketing strategy:

• Situation Analysis:

Lead a careful investigation of your business climate. Examine internal factors (strengths, weaknesses) and external factors (opportunities, threats) to identify key insights.

• Define Marketing Objectives:

Clearly outline specific, measurable, achievable, relevant, and time-bound (SMART) marketing objectives. These ought to line up with your general business objectives.

• Target Audience Identification:

Define your target audience based on demographics, psychographics, and behavior. While making designated advertising messages, understanding your interest group is fundamental.

• Competitor Analysis:

Analyze competitors to identify their strengths and weaknesses. Decide open doors for separation and methodologies to outflank rivals.

• SWOT Analysis:

Distinguish your business' assets, shortcomings, potential open doors, and dangers. Utilize these bits of knowledge to illuminate your showcasing system and gain by qualities while alleviating shortcomings.

• Positioning Strategy:

Develop a clear positioning strategy that communicates your unique value proposition. Feature what separates your image on the lookout.

• Marketing Mix (4 Ps):

Define your product or service offerings (Product), determine your pricing strategy (Price), outline distribution channels (Place), and plan promotional activities (Promotion).

• Budget Allocation:

Distribute a spending plan for each showcasing drive. Focus on high-influence systems and guarantee a harmony among on the web and disconnected channels.

• Marketing Channels:

Select appropriate marketing channels based on your target audience. Consider digital channels (social media, email marketing) and traditional channels (print, events) for a holistic approach.

• Content Strategy:

Foster a substance system that lines up with your image voice and reverberates with your crowd. Make important, shareable substances across different stages.

• Social Media Plan:

Craft a social media strategy outlining the platforms you'll use, content calendars, and engagement tactics. Leverage social media for brand awareness and community building.

• **SEO and SEM Strategy:**

Implement a robust Search Engine Optimization (SEO) strategy for organic visibility. Supplement with Search Engine Marketing (SEM) for targeted paid campaigns.

• **Email Marketing Campaigns:**

Develop targeted email campaigns for lead generation, nurturing, and customer retention. Customize content to upgrade commitment.

• **Measurement and Analytics:**

Establish key performance indicators (KPIs) for each marketing initiative. Use examination apparatuses to quantify and investigate crusade execution, making information driven changes.

• **Timeline and Milestones:**

Create a detailed timeline with milestones for each marketing initiative. Clearly define deadlines and responsibilities to ensure timely execution.

• Risk Management:

Identify potential risks and develop contingency plans. Expecting difficulties mitigates adverse consequences on your advertising plan.

• Team Collaboration:

Encourage cooperation among promoting and different divisions. Guarantee arrangement with in general business techniques and steady correspondence.

• Regular Review and Adjustment:

Schedule regular reviews of your marketing plan. Dissect execution information, look for input, and make vital changes in accordance with upgrade results.

By fastidiously tending to every component of your promoting plan, you can make a guide that lines up with your business goals, draws in your interest group, and adjusts to the powerful idea of the market.

Chapter 6: Effective Marketing Strategies

Creating viable promoting procedures is fundamental for organizations meaning to reach and connect with their interest group. Here's a detailed guide to help you develop impactful marketing strategies:

• **Market Segmentation:**

Partition your objective market into fragments in light of socio economics, psychographics, and conduct. Tailor your advertising messages to address the particular necessities and inclinations of each portion.

• **Unique Value Proposition (UVP):**

Clearly define your Unique Value Proposition – what sets your product or service apart from competitors. Communicate this distinctiveness consistently across all marketing channels.

• In-depth Customer Persona Development:

Create detailed customer personas to understand your audience on a deeper level making it easier to personalize and target marketing efforts.

• Content Marketing:

Develop a robust content marketing strategy. Make superior grades, significant substances that teach, engage, or tackle issues for your crowd. This structures trust and positions your picture as a power.

• Social Media Engagement:

Leverage social media platforms strategically and engage with your audience, share useful content, run targeted ads, and take part in pertinent conversations to boost your brand's visibility.

• Influencer Marketing:

Work together with powerhouses in your industry or specialty. Forces to be reckoned with can give valid support and essentially extend your range to their adherents.

• SEO Optimization:

Invest in Search Engine Optimization (SEO) to enhance your online visibility. Enhance site content, utilize applicable watchwords, and fabricate quality backlinks to further develop web search tool rankings.

• Email Marketing Automation:

Implement email marketing automation for personalized and timely communication. Utilize portioned records and computerization arrangements to sustain leads and hold clients.

- **User-Generated Content (UGC):**

Urge your clients to make and share content connected with your image. UGC fabricates legitimacy, connects with your local area, and fills in as significant social confirmation.

- **Referral Programs:**

Develop referral programs to incentivize existing customers to refer others. Also word-of-mouth marketing is powerful and can lead to a network effect.

- **Loyalty Programs:**

Lay out devotion projects to compensate for rehashing clients. This increments client maintenance as well as supports brand backing.

- **Partnerships and Collaborations:**

Form strategic partnerships with other businesses or influencers in complementary industries. Cooperative endeavors can extend your compass and acquaint your image with new crowds.

• Interactive Content:

Create interactive content such as quizzes, polls, or contests because it helps connect with your audience and provides important information for future advertising experiences.

• Data Analytics and Measurement:

Use data analytics tools to measure the effectiveness of your marketing efforts. Analyze key performance indicators (KPIs) and adjust strategies based on the insights gained.

• Omni-channel Marketing:

Implement an omni-channel marketing approach for a seamless customer experience across various touchpoints. Brand trust and recognition are boosted by consistency.

• Adaptability and Innovation:

Stay agile and open to innovation. Regularly assess market trends, consumer behaviors, and emerging technologies. Adjust your systems to remain ahead in a unique scene.

• Customer Feedback Integration:

Actively seek and incorporate customer feedback. This not just empowers you to improve your items or administrations yet in addition fortifies your relationship with clients.

• Emotional Branding:

Connect with your audience on an emotional level.
Put forth advancing attempts that bring good sentiments, empowering a more significant relationship with your picture.

Putting these systems into your showing plan, you can make an exhaustive and reasonable methodology that resounds with your gathering and drives basic outcomes for your business.

Navigating the basics of marketing

Embarking on the journey of Navigating the Basics of Marketing is akin to charting the course for your business's triumphant voyage into the hearts and minds of your audience. Start by plunging into the profundities of statistical surveying, enlightening the neglected subtleties of your industry and figuring out the cadence of your rivals.

Create an orchestra of words that frames your one of a kind incentive, reverberating through the immense territory of purchaser scenes. Your essential showcasing plan turns into the compass, directing your vessel through the constantly changing flows of crowd inclinations and industry patterns.

Hoist the sails of a multi-channel approach, catching the winds of social media, content creation, and targeted emails. Let each platform be a stage for your brand's performance, with tailored messages that resonate like a harmonious melody.

Optimize your digital flagship, your website, ensuring it stands tall on the SEO horizon. Social media becomes your amphitheater, where engagement becomes a dance with your audience, and each post is a note in the symphony of your brand story.

Project your publicizing nets all over, investigating the profundities of both web-based domains and conventional roads. As the captain of your ship, analyze the stars of analytics to steer your course, ensuring every marketing endeavor is a calculated and purposeful move.

In the vast sea of customer relations, let your CRM be the anchor that holds steadfast. Weather storms of feedback gracefully, shaping your business's evolution with each customer interaction.

Make your excursion a common undertaking by working with industry leaders and friends.Go to the advertising celebrations and systems administration ports, fashioning coalitions that will fortify your presence in unknown regions.

As you leave on special journeys, offer limits as fortunes, drawing in new team individuals while guaranteeing the dedication of your carefully prepared benefactors.

In this grand narrative of marketing, every promotion is a plot twist, keeping the audience eagerly anticipating the next chapter.

In this odyssey, let the winds of innovation carry your ship forward. Bridle the force of narrating to wind around stories that enrapture hearts and make a strong connection among brand and shopper. As you navigate through the seas of competition, be vigilant, adapting your course as needed, and staying ahead in the race.

With a ship fueled by data-driven insights, captained by creativity, and crewed by customer-centricity, you're not just navigating the basics of marketing — you're orchestrating a symphony that resonates with audiences, creating waves that leave an indelible mark on the vast ocean of consumer consciousness. Set sail with confidence, for in navigating the basics of marketing, you're crafting an epic tale of brand success.

As your advertising odyssey unfurls, peer into the star groupings of information, removing experiences that enlighten the most obscure corners of buyer conduct. Let your ship of strategies be adaptable, embracing the winds of change and evolving with the tides of market dynamics.

Enhance your substance stockpile, utilizing words as well as a lively cluster of visuals, infographics, and intelligent components. Change your story into a vivid encounter, leaving a permanent engraving on the personalities of your crowd.

As you sail through the vast seas of competition, keep a watchful eye on the tactics of fellow captains. Analyze their maneuvers, not just as competitors but as sources of inspiration and lessons for your own marketing playbook.

Engage not just in marketing but in a communal dance with your audience. Attend to the beats of community engagement, sponsoring local events, and forging connections that transform customers into advocates. Your brand doesn't just exist; it resonates within the heartbeats of the community.

In the symphony of customer service, let each interaction be a note of harmony. Respond promptly, address concerns with finesse, and let each customer feel like a VIP passenger on the journey of your brand.

Investigate the unexplored marketing technologies. Adventure into the domains of computerized reasoning, chatbots, and robotization, changing your boat into a vessel that sails as well as takes off on the forefront of development.

The voyage of marketing is not solitary but a collaborative expedition. Form alliances not just within your industry but across borders. The excursion becomes more extravagant when shared, as different points of view and organizations impel your boat farther than any solitary vessel could go.

In your marketing epic, remain agile, swift in adjusting your sails to the winds of change. Whether it's a shift in consumer tastes or a storm of market disruptions, your ability to adapt ensures not just survival but triumph in the face of adversity.

So, let your marketing voyage be not just a navigation of basics but an exploration of the extraordinary. In each marketing endeavor, see not just a task but an opportunity to craft a narrative that captivates, a strategy that resonates, and a brand that stands the test of time. As you navigate the basics of marketing, remember: this is not just a journey; it's a saga, and the story you tell will be written in the hearts of your audience. Sail on, intrepid marketer, and let your legacy be one of brilliance and enduring success.

Online and offline marketing tactics

Exploring the powerful domain of promoting requires a complete methodology that flawlessly coordinates both on the web and disconnected strategies, making a synergistic methodology that resounds across different channels.

Online Marketing Tactics:

• Digital Presence Optimization:

Your website is the virtual storefront, and optimizing it for search engines (SEO) ensures it's easily discoverable. Make a consistent web-based section point by creating an easy to understand experience that changes over guests into clients.

• Social Media Engagement:

Social platforms are vibrant stages for your brand's performance. Connect with your crowd through convincing substance, utilizing the intelligent idea of stages like Facebook, Instagram, and Twitter to construct a local area around your image.

• Digital Advertising Campaigns:

Dive into the digital advertising seas with strategies like Google Ads and social media campaigns. Targeted advertisements will spread your message to the vast online landscape and boost traffic to your digital domain as well.

• Email Marketing:

Email campaigns are personalized narratives, reaching directly into the inboxes of your audience. Make significant messages that resound, sustaining connections and encouraging brand faithfulness through cautiously organized content.

Offline Marketing Tactics:

• Event Marketing:

Physical events provide tangible touchpoints for your brand. Whether it's a career expo, meeting, or nearby occasion, eye to eye communications make enduring impressions and fabricate connections past the computerized circle.

• Traditional Advertising:

Embrace classic methods such as print and radio advertising. Unmistakable and immortal, these channels permit your image to hang out in a world frequently soaked with computerized clamor, making a paramount effect.

• Networking and Partnerships:

Offline networking is a voyage into the heart of industry connections. Fabricate joint efforts and associations through eye to eye corporations, producing connections that reach out past virtual stages.

• Brick-and-Mortar Experience:

For businesses with physical locations, the ambiance, customer service, and overall in-store experience become vital components of the marketing narrative. Make a paramount environment that supplements your image story.

Harmonizing the Symphony:

The power of an effective marketing strategy lies in the seamless integration of both online and offline tactics. It's not a matter of choosing one over the other but orchestrating a symphony where each instrument plays a crucial role.

Online strategies influence the tremendous reach and intelligent nature of the advanced scene, while disconnected strategies give unmistakable, human associations that improve brand trust. The best promoting procedures track down the fragile harmony among pixels and obviousness, making a story that reverberates across all elements of the shopper venture. In this agreeable mix, your image's story turns into an enamoring song, leaving an enduring engraving on your crowd.

Crafting a successful marketing plan

To leave on this excursion, begin with a thorough market examination. Investigating socioeconomics, tendencies, and behavior will help you learn about your target audience. Simultaneously, evaluate your competitors and industry trends to identify opportunities and potential challenges.

Characterize a convincing Extraordinary Selling Recommendation (USP) that plainly imparts what separates your business. Your brand's identity and message will be built on top of this distinctiveness. Once you've established your USP, set specific and measurable marketing goals. Whether your focus is on building brand awareness, generating leads, or driving sales, having clear objectives will guide your efforts.

Make individualized messages that resonate with various customer groups by segmenting your target audience. Utilize a mix of marketing channels based on where your audience is most active.

Computerized stages, web-based entertainment, content advertising, and customary channels all assume special parts in coming to and drawing in your objective market.

Foster a steady and noteworthy brand personality across all touchpoints. It incorporates your image's character, tones, informing, and logo. Consistency constructs trust and builds up memorability.

Allocate your marketing budget strategically, prioritizing high-impact strategies aligned with your goals. Remember how important it is to take a variety of approaches that allow for experimentation and performance data-based optimization.

Routinely screen and examine the presentation of your advertising endeavors.

Logical devices can be utilized to find out about what's working and what can be gotten to the next level. these discoveries, showing nimbleness because of the powerful idea of the market.

Cultivate client commitment by making intuitive substance, carrying out criticism instruments, and giving customized encounters. Building major areas of strength for a with your crowd upgrades brand devotion and supports rehash business.

Adaptability is significant in the continually moving promoting scene. Remain sensitive to industry changes, arising patterns, and advancing customer ways of behaving. Persistently refine your advertising systems to remain in front of the opposition and guarantee supported achievement. Keep in mind, at the center of your endeavors ought to be the conveyance of significant worth to your crowd, encouraging enduring associations and driving long haul business development.

Dive deeper into your market analysis by conducting a SWOT analysis (Strengths, Weaknesses, Opportunities, Threats). Making this essential evaluation will assist you with benefiting from inward qualities, address shortcomings, immediately jump all over chances, and relieve likely dangers.

When segmenting your target audience, go beyond demographics and psychographics. Consider factors, for example, purchaser personas, venture planning, and client lifecycle stages. Fitting your information to line up with these subtleties improves the pertinence and effect of your showcasing endeavors.

Investigate the force of powerhouse showcasing and associations. Working together with powerhouses or reciprocal organizations can enhance your range and believability. Guarantee that these coordinated efforts line up with your image esteems and reverberate with your crowd.

Incorporate customer feedback and testimonials into your marketing strategy. Positive surveys and tributes act as strong social verification, building trust and believability. Actively encourage and showcase customer success stories to strengthen your brand reputation.

Embrace information driven direction by utilizing examination apparatuses. Track key performance indicators (KPIs) across various marketing channels to measure ROI effectively. You can improve crusades, refine systems, and distribute assets where they have the best contact with this information driven approach.

Contemplate how experiential advertising can assist you with making your crowd's corporations essential.Whether through events, product demonstrations, or immersive online experiences, fostering a personal connection enhances brand recall and loyalty.

Remain informed about arising advances and patterns in your industry. Incorporate innovative approaches such as augmented reality, artificial intelligence, or interactive content to stay ahead of the curve and captivate your audience in new and exciting ways.

Chapter 7: Operations and Management

In the powerful scene of tasks, the idea of store network flexibility becomes vital. Past advancing associations with providers, executing alternate courses of action for interruptions, like cataclysmic events or international occasions, is pivotal. Foster a broadened provider base to relieve gambles, guaranteeing a versatile inventory network that can endure unexpected difficulties.

Investigate agile methodologies within the context of project management. Light-footed standards make versatility, coordinated effort, and adaptability main concerns. Subsequently, groups can rapidly answer changes in project necessities. Integrating nimble philosophies into your functional system advances an iterative turn of events, improving your group's capacity to convey great outcomes productively.

Think about the job of information security and protection in your functional methodology. As organizations progressively depend on information, it is central to shield delicate data. Execute strong network safety measures, comply with information assurance guidelines, and consistently review your security conventions to safeguard both client and hierarchical information.

Explore the idea of round economy rehearses with regards to tasks. Plan items and cycles with an emphasis on maintainability, intending to limit squander and broaden the life expectancy of items. Embracing roundabout economy standards adds to natural protection as well as lines up with advancing customer inclinations for eco-accommodating organizations.

Investigate the mix of computerized reasoning (man-made intelligence) and AI (ML) in tasks. Man-made intelligence and ML advancements can upgrade processes, robotize routine errands, and give important bits of knowledge through prescient examination. Study the pertinence of these advances to work on autonomous heading, capability, and all around utilitarian execution.

Inside activities, dig into the universe of client experience the board.Past conveying an item or administration, focus on the general client venture.

These incorporate understanding client touchpoints, gathering input, and diligently refining cycles to further develop the overall client experience. A positive client experience adds to check dedication and backing.

Contemplate the occupation of cross-useful collaboration in exercises. Destroy departmental storehouses to make cooperation and correspondence more straightforward. Drawing in cross-significant social events upgrades unequivocal thinking cutoff points and raises a comprehensive strategy for overseeing commonsense difficulties.

To increment functional effectiveness, research the chance of rethinking insignificant assignments.Your group can focus on its center skills while using outside mastery for specific undertakings because of this essential decision. Assess re-appropriating open doors in regions, for example, IT administrations, client service, or assembling.

Analyze the effect of corporate culture on activities. make a positive and comprehensive working environment culture that cultivates cooperation, development, and representative fulfillment. A solid hierarchical culture adds to higher worker confidence, efficiency, and generally speaking functional achievement.

Dive into the domain of nonstop improvement systems, like Six Sigma or Kaizen. All these methodologies center around distinguishing and disposing of deformities or shortcomings in processes. Carrying out ceaseless improvement drives encourages a culture of greatness and drives continuous functional upgrades.

Put into consideration the job of web-based entertainment in tasks, especially in client commitment and brand building. Use social stages to interface with your crowd, assemble input, and address client requests. Web-based entertainment likewise fills in as a significant device for brand advancement and mindfulness.

Evaluate the idea of adaptive leadership in management. Versatile pioneers are receptive to change, equipped for exploring vulnerability, and proficient at directing their groups through powerful circumstances. Cultivate versatile authority inside your supervisory crew to successfully control the association through advancing difficulties.

Analyze the capability of representative strengthening in administration techniques. Empowered specialists feel a deep satisfaction and commitment, inciting extended motivation and proficiency. Consolidate strengthening drives, for example, independence in navigation and potential open doors for proficient development.

Think about the job of the capacity to appreciate anyone on a profound level in viable administration. Pioneers with high capacity to appreciate people on a deeper level can explore relational elements, construct solid connections, and grasp the feelings of their colleagues. Putting resources into the improvement of the capacity to understand individuals on a deeper level among the board upgrades initiative viability.

Investigate the idea of groundbreaking initiative inside administration rehearses. Groundbreaking pioneers rouse and spur their groups to accomplish past assumptions. Breed a groundbreaking initiative style that encourages coordinated effort, imagination, and development.

With regards to the board, investigate the capability of working environment adaptability and remote work arrangements. The advanced labor force values adaptability, and associations that embrace remote work choices show a comprehension of developing work inclinations. Employee satisfaction and retention are aided by flexible work schedules.

Think about the effect of variety and incorporation drives on administration. Different groups bring different viewpoints and thoughts, cultivating imagination and advancement. Lay out comprehensive administration rehearses that advance variety and make a work environment where all people feel esteemed and heard.

Investigate the idea of authoritative advancing inside administration. Cultivate a culture of constant realizing where workers are urged to obtain new abilities and information. Lay out preparing programs, mentorship drives, and information sharing stages to help continuous expert turn of events.

Analyze the job of progress the board in authoritative achievement. Teams will easily adapt to new strategies, technologies, or processes if change initiatives are managed well. Executing vigorous change the board rehearses upgrades hierarchical spryness and flexibility.

Ponder about the effect of moral authority on hierarchical culture. Moral pioneers set a norm for respectability, straightforwardness, and capable independent direction. Integrate moral authority standards into the board practices to fabricate trust among workers, clients, and different partners.

Focus on the task of leadership advancement. Foster a culture that engages and compensates imaginative reasoning. Make channels for the change of imaginative ideas into substantial arrangements, assess the feasibility of carrying out new innovations, and lay out systems for the age of novel ideas.

By examining these extended thoughts in the two undertakings and the board, you foster a total and crucial system that positions your relationship for upheld result in the complicated and propelling scene of business.

Setting up efficient business operations

Setting up powerful business errands is an establishment for reasonable turn of events and accomplishment. Start by obviously characterizing your business targets and objectives. This lucidity gives a guide to planning functional cycles that line up with your overall system.

Direct a cautious assessment of your industry and market to get a handle on key examples, client tendencies, and relentless scenes. It makes your important choices clear, ensuring that they are tailored to meet the particular requirements of your best vested party.

Lay out obvious and recorded processes for every part of your business, from item/administration conveyance to client care and inside correspondence. Making sense of strategies help to streamline exercises, increase liability, and lessen dubiousness.

Put resources into development that meet your company's needs.Using innovation works on in general proficiency, lessens mistakes, and mechanizes routine undertakings in all that from projecting the board devices to CRM frameworks.Consider versatile arrangements that can develop with your business.

Give employee development and training top priority. Thoroughly prepared workers are more prepared to deal with their jobs productively, lessening blunders and supporting generally speaking efficiency. Execute progressing preparing projects to keep your group side by side of industry drifts and developing prescribed procedures.

Smooth out correspondence channels inside your association. Whether through cooperative apparatuses, customary gatherings, or venture the executives stages, compelling correspondence is fundamental for facilitated and effective business activities. make a culture of transparent correspondence.

Carry out key execution pointers (KPIs) to quantify the adequacy of your tasks. Consistently screen these measurements to distinguish regions for development, improve processes, and guarantee that your business is on target to meet its goals. Information driven bits of knowledge add to informed direction.

Consider re-appropriating non-center capabilities to particular specialist co-ops. fundamentally this move promotes practical efficiency and cost-effectiveness by allowing your group to concentrate on focus skills while external experts handle unambiguous tasks.

Lay out a powerful production network and the executives framework. Make relationships with strong suppliers, smooth out stock levels, and complete compelling composed tasks. A very much oversaw production network guarantees a consistent progression of materials and lessens the gamble of disturbances.

Coordinate client criticism circles into your activities. Effectively look for input from clients, investigate their inclinations, and utilize this data to refine items/administrations and functional cycles. Client driven tasks add to higher fulfillment and steadfastness.

Fabricate a culture of nonstop improvement inside your association. Urge representatives to distinguish shortcomings, propose upgrades, and partake in critical thinking. This obligation to steady progress guarantees that your business practices make sense with creating conditions.

Think about the reception of supportable and harmless ecosystems. In addition to the fact that this lines up with developing customer inclinations, however it likewise adds to cost reserve funds and long haul business strength.

Routinely audit and update your functional cycles. Advance your business as well as your activities. Lead occasional appraisals to recognize obsolete practices, consolidate new innovations, and guarantee that your tasks stay lithe and versatile.

Burn through cash on successful organization safety efforts to defend delicate information and keep up with the reliability of your errands. Complete encryption, secure access controls, and reliably update security shows to safeguard your business from likely advanced risks.

Lay out an alternate course of action for unanticipated disturbances. Whether catastrophic events, monetary slumps, or worldwide occasions, having a thoroughly examined emergency course of action guarantees that your business can adjust and keep working under testing conditions.

Advance cross-practical joint effort. Separate storehouses among divisions and empower coordinated effort among groups. It encourages an all encompassing comprehension of the business and empowers representatives to work solidly toward shared objectives.

Screen industry drifts and arising advancements. Find any new developments that might help your company. Embracing new innovations and systems positions your business at the front line of proficiency and versatility.

Consistently evaluate the adaptability of your activities. Ensure that your foundation and cycles can develop with you without forfeiting proficiency. Versatile tasks give an establishment a long haul achievement.

Spread out a culture of responsibility in your association. Obviously characterize jobs and obligations, set execution assumptions, and consider people responsible for their commitments. Responsibility advances a feeling of pride and obligation, driving functional greatness.

Via cautiously considering and carrying out these methodologies, you lay the preparation for setting up proficient business tasks that are versatile, client centered, and designed for long haul progress in a cutthroat business climate.

Human resources and team building

Human resources and group building assume significant parts in molding the hierarchical culture, driving representative commitment, and encouraging a cooperative workplace. Beginning with HR, it fills in as the foundation of the ability of the executives, from enlistment to worker improvement and maintenance.

• Strategic Workforce Planning:

HR begins with strategic workforce planning, aligning the organization's objectives with its human capital needs. By gauging future ability necessities, HR guarantees that the perfect individuals are in the ideal jobs at the ideal time.

• Enlistment and Determination:

A hearty enrollment process is fundamental for drawing in top ability. To guarantee that up-and-comers are a decent counterpart for the association's qualities and targets, HR experts foster effective enrollment methodologies, direct meetings, and assess competitors.

• Onboarding and Orientation:

Successful onboarding sets the tone for an employee's journey. HR works with complete onboarding projects to incorporate fresh recruits flawlessly into the authoritative culture, giving the essential devices and data for progress.

• Employee Training and Development:

HR plays a key role in identifying skill gaps and organizing training programs to enhance employee capabilities. Nonstop learning potential open doors add to worker fulfillment and hierarchical development.

• Performance Management:

HR establishes performance management systems to set expectations, provide feedback, and recognize achievements. Workers gain a superior comprehension of their assets and regions for development through standard execution surveys.

• Compensation and Benefits:

Developing competitive compensation packages and attractive benefits is crucial for talent retention. HR professionals regularly review and adjust these offerings to remain competitive in the job market.

• Employee Relations:

HR acts as a mediator in resolving conflicts and fostering positive employee relations. Open correspondence channels guarantee that workers feel appreciated and upheld in their expert process.

• Workplace Diversity and Inclusion:

HR is instrumental in promoting diversity and inclusion initiatives. Making a different labor force encourages development, inventiveness, and a more extensive point of view inside the association.

• Employee Engagement:

HR designs initiatives to enhance employee engagement, recognizing that engaged employees are more likely to be productive and committed to the company's success.

• Wellness Programs:

HR may implement wellness programs to prioritize employee health and well-being. It adds to a positive working environment and diminishing delinquency.

Moving on to team building:

• Team Formation:

Effective team building starts with assembling the right mix of skills and personalities. Taking into account each person's strengths and weaknesses, human resources help form teams that are well-balanced.

• Team Building Activities:

Organizing team-building activities fosters collaboration and strengthens interpersonal relationships. These exercises can go from studios and retreats to relaxed group excursions.

• Communication Training:

HR invests in communication training to ensure that team members can express themselves clearly and understand each other. The foundation of successful team dynamics is clear communication.

• Conflict Resolution:

Team building also involves equipping teams with conflict resolution skills. HR gives preparation and assets to address clashes usefully and keep a sound group climate.

• Leadership Development:

HR identifies and nurtures leadership potential within teams. Leadership Programs for further developing organization add to individuals' development and the gathering's general practicality.

• Goal Setting and Alignment:

Group building incorporates adjusting individual and group objectives to hierarchical goals. Goal-setting sessions are facilitated by HR to ensure that everyone is working toward the same objectives.

• Recognition and Rewards:

Recognizing and rewarding team achievements is crucial for morale and motivation. The frameworks for recognizing exceptional collaboration and individual commitment are laid out in human resources.

• Collaborative Tools:

HR introduces collaborative tools and technologies to enhance communication and streamline teamwork. Instances of these instruments incorporate stages for projecting the board, applications for conveying, and virtual spaces for joint effort.

• Regular Feedback:

Team building involves creating a culture of continuous improvement. HR works with standard criticism meetings and empowers open correspondence in regards to qualities and shortcomings.

• Cross-Functional Collaboration:

HR promotes cross-functional collaboration by breaking down silos between departments. Empowering groups to team up across capabilities encourages an all encompassing way to deal with critical thinking.

• Empowerment:

Team building emphasizes empowering team members to take ownership of their work. HR energizes a feeling of obligation and independence, adding to a more connected with and self-propelled group.

• Cultural Alignment:

HR ensures that team members are aligned with the organizational culture. This includes imparting guiding principles and cultivating a climate where everybody feels a feeling of having a place.

• Innovation Initiatives:

Team building extends to fostering a culture of innovation. HR urges get-togethers to think innovatively, share considerations, and add to the connection's reliable improvement.

• Adaptability Training:

In a rapidly changing business landscape, HR emphasizes adaptability within teams. Training in adapting to change, overcoming obstacles, and remaining resilient are all part of this.

• Inclusive Decision-Making:

Team building incorporates inclusive decision-making processes. Human resources makes sure that different points of view are taken in the same direction, which makes for more powerful and balanced results.

• Social Events:

Beyond formal team-building activities, HR may organize social events to facilitate informal interactions. These occasions add to building brotherhood and a feeling of local area inside the group.

• Mentorship Programs:

HR may implement mentorship programs to facilitate knowledge transfer and professional growth within the team. Pairing experienced team members with those seeking guidance promotes a collaborative learning environment.

• Celebrating Milestones:

Acknowledging and celebrating team milestones is an essential aspect of team building. To cultivate a positive and supportive team culture, HR coordinates efforts to recognize accomplishments.

• Team Diversity and Inclusion:

Just as in HR, team building emphasizes the importance of diversity and inclusion. Creating different groups advances points of view and adds to more creative critical thinking.

• Continuous Evaluation:

Team building is an ongoing process. HR routinely assesses the adequacy of group building drives, requesting criticism from colleagues and making any fundamental changes.

The cooperative energy among HR and group building is essential to making a working environment where people flourish, team up really, and add to the general progress of the association. Ceaseless interest in the two regions guarantees that the labor force stays drawn in, persuaded, and lined up with the organization's central goal and values.

Day-to-day management tips

Feasible ordinary organization is essential for staying aware of effectiveness, developing a positive work environment, and achieving progressive targets. Here are some practical day-to-day management tips to enhance efficiency and effectiveness:

• Prioritize Tasks:

Begin each day by identifying and prioritizing tasks. By focusing on high-priority tasks that are in line with the goals of the organization, essential goals will always be met.

• Time Blocking:

Allocate specific blocks of time for different types of tasks. It dodges performing multiple tasks, further develops fixation, and takes into consideration more effective utilization of time.

• Effective Communication:

Clearly communicate expectations, goals, and any changes to the team.Cultivate an entryway strategy, empowering colleagues to offer their viewpoints and concerns.

• Regular Check-ins:

Schedule regular check-ins with team members to discuss progress, address challenges, and provide support. These gatherings can be brief yet add to a straightforward and cooperative workplace.

• Set Realistic Goals:

Establish achievable and realistic goals for yourself and your team. Having an unrealistic expectation can lead to stress and decreased morale.

• Delegate Admirably:

Agent assignments in view of colleagues' assets and abilities. Effective delegation empowers team members, distributes workload evenly, and promotes skill development.

• Use Task Management Tools:

Leverage task management tools and apps to organize and track tasks. You can use these devices to stay composed, set cutoff times, and screen progress.

• Handle Email Strategically:

Avoid constant email interruptions by setting specific times to check and respond to emails. It forestalls interruptions and takes into consideration more engaged work periods.

• Embrace Technology:

Utilize technology to streamline processes. Robotization, project executive programming, and joint effort apparatuses can upgrade proficiency and correspondence.

• Encourage Breaks:

Recognize the importance of breaks to maintain productivity and prevent burnout. Encourage team members to take short breaks to refresh and recharge.

• Flexibility and Adaptability:

Be flexible and adaptable to changes in priorities or unexpected challenges. Changes and solutions can be found quickly with a flexible approach.

• Conflict Resolution:

Address conflicts promptly and constructively. Provide a platform for open communication, assist in the resolution of disputes when necessary, and encourage a collaborative approach to the process.

• Consistent Learning:

Cultivate a culture of ceaseless learning. Remain refreshed on industry patterns, urge colleagues to look for a proficient turn of events, and offer information inside the group.

• Employee Recognition:

Recognize and celebrate achievements regularly. Recognizing achievements makes everyone feel significantly better and spurs the group.

• Mindful Decision-Making:

Take the time to make thoughtful and informed decisions. Think about expected results, include pertinent partners, and survey the drawn out effect of decisions.

• Energize Coordinated effort:

Advance a cooperative climate where colleagues can share thoughts, give input, and work together on projects. Joint exertion develops improvement and a sensation of fortitude.

• Promote Work-Life Balance:

Encourage a healthy work-life balance among team members. Recognize the importance of personal time and ensure that constant work demands do not lead to burnout.

• Document Processes:

Maintain clear documentation of processes and procedures. This documentation fills in as a wellspring of point of view for the gathering, ensures consistency, and works with getting ready.

• Manage Meetings Effectively:

Keep meetings focused, set agendas in advance, and involve only necessary participants. Meetings can be used as a way to work together and make decisions.

• Regularly Review and Reflect:

Take time at the end of each day to review accomplishments, assess challenges, and plan for the next day. Reflection on a regular basis aids in continuous improvement.

• Encourage Feedback:

Create a feedback loop where team members can provide input on processes, projects, and team dynamics.To further develop frameworks and encourage a culture of progress, helpful information is urgent.

• Advance a Positive Culture:

Encourage a positive and comprehensive working environment culture. See achievements, advance fellowship, and assurance that the work environment is useful for specialist thriving.

• Engage Colleagues:

Engage colleagues to take responsibility for work. Give open doors to expertise improvement, independence, and decision-production to impart a feeling of obligation.

• Be Accessible:

Maintain open lines of communication and be accessible to team members.Transparency helps construct trust and urges partners to search for bearing when required.

• Celebrate Milestones:

Acknowledge and celebrate both individual and team milestones. Merriments develop a pride and push the gathering to make a pass at significance.

• Set Clear Expectations:

Clearly communicate expectations regarding roles, responsibilities, and project deliverables. Setting clear expectations reduce confusion and encourage accountability.

• Promote Wellness Initiatives:

Implement wellness initiatives that support the physical and mental well-being of team members. These drives add to a superior and more associated with the workforce.

• Remain Coordinated:

Keep a coordinated work area and computerized climate.It adds to adequacy, lessens tension, and ensures that fundamental information is truly open.

• Persistent Improvement:

Encourage a culture of ceaseless improvement. Ask associates to propose moves up to processes, share delineations learned, and actually participate in refining exercises.

• Lead by Example:

Demonstrate the qualities you expect from your team. Show others how its done concerning hard working attitude, correspondence, and a promise to the association's qualities.

By integrating these everyday administration tips into your initiative methodology, you make an establishment for a very much made due, inspired, and high-performing group, adding to the general outcome of your association.

Chapter 8: Financial Management

Monetary administration involves arranging, sorting out, planning, and controlling an association's monetary resources to accomplish its objectives.It includes a scope of exercises pointed toward upgrading the utilization of assets, guaranteeing benefit, and supporting long haul monetary wellbeing. It affects each degree of decision-production since it covers an extensive variety of business tasks. Financial management is a significant piece of keeping a strong business, including basic preparation, organizing, and seeing cash related execution.

Here are key considerations in financial management:

• Budgeting:

Develop a comprehensive budget that outlines expected revenues and expenditures. Regularly review and adjust the budget to align with business goals.

• Cash Flow Management:

Monitor cash flow to ensure there's enough liquidity for day-to-day operations. Successful income from the board is crucial for business maintainability.

• Financial Planning:

Create a strategic financial plan that aligns with long-term business objectives. This plan should harden speculation systems, improvement plans, and chance affiliation.

• Risk The board:

Distinguish likely monetary dangers and carry out techniques to alleviate them. It integrates widening hypotheses, having security incorporation, and staying informed about market designs.

•Financial Analysis:

Regularly analyze financial statements, including income statements, balance sheets, and cash flow statements. Doing this gives snippets of data into the monetary strength and position of the business.

• Cost Control:

Implement cost-control measures to optimize expenses without compromising quality. Regularly review operational costs and seek ways to improve efficiency.

• Investment Decisions:

Make informed investment decisions based on risk-return analyses. Consider the expected effect on income, benefit, and long haul development.

• Credit Management:

Manage credit effectively, both in terms of extending credit to customers and handling business credit. Monitor receivables closely to minimize the risk of bad debts.

• Financial Reporting:

Ensure accurate and timely financial reporting. Straightforward revealing is vital for keeping up with entrust with partners, including financial backers, loan bosses, and administrative bodies.

•Tax Planning:

Engage in strategic tax planning to optimize the business's tax position. Comply with tax regulations and take advantage of incentives that are available.

• Cost of Capital:

Understand the cost of obtaining funds for the business, whether through equity or debt. Evaluate different financing options to minimize the overall cost of capital.

• Working Capital Management:

Effectively manage working capital by balancing current assets and liabilities. It guarantees smooth everyday activities and limits the requirement for outer funding.

• Financial Forecasting:

Develop financial forecasts to anticipate future trends and potential challenges. It supports proactive independent direction and asset distribution.

• Profitability Analysis:

Analyze profitability by assessing profit margins, return on investment, and other key performance indicators. The information gotten guides systems for further developing efficiency.

• Capital Structure Optimization:

Optimize the capital structure by finding the right balance between equity and debt. The cost of capital and financial stability are affected by this.

• Dividend Policy:

Establish a clear dividend policy that aligns with the business's financial goals. Consider reinvesting profits for growth or distributing dividends to shareholders.

• Auditing and Compliance:

Conduct regular internal audits to ensure financial processes adhere to regulations and organizational policies. Consistence with money related standards is critical for legitimate and moral reasons.

• Currency Management (if applicable):

If dealing with international transactions, manage currency risks effectively. Consider using support systems to safeguard against conversion scale changes.

• Financial Education:

Ensure key stakeholders, including management and employees, have a basic understanding of financial principles. Monetary proficiency adds to informed independent direction.

• Continuous Improvement:

Embrace a culture of continuous improvement in financial management practices. Reconsider procedures routinely, look for amazing open doors for effectiveness, and adjust to changes in the business climate.

Ceaseless observing, assessment, and change are vital for a powerful way to deal with monetary administration.Via completing these norms, associations can investigate financial hardships and work toward practical turn of events and accomplishment.

Budgeting and financial planning

Making money related plans incorporates spreading out financial goals, evaluating what's going on, and making an aide for achieving those targets. It wraps different parts, including retirement orchestrating, saving, risk the board, and attainable money related arranging. The fundamental objective of financial orchestrating is to ensure that individuals, associations, or affiliations can meet their money related targets, both for the present and long stretch, while investigating weaknesses and progressing available resources.

Planning and monetary arranging are the underpinnings of a sound financial method, essential for individuals and affiliations the equivalent. The management of assets, achieving financial goals, and investigation of the complexities of financial scenes are all outlined in these practices.

• Foundation of Financial Success:

At its core, budgeting and financial planning serve as the foundation for financial success. Carefully allocating resources, individuals and businesses can establish a clear path toward achieving short-term objectives and long-term aspirations.

• Strategic Goal Setting:

Effective financial planning involves setting clear and strategic financial goals. Whether it's saving for a home, funding education, or expanding a business, articulating specific objectives provides direction and purpose.

• Income and Expense Alignment:

Budgeting allows for a structured approach to aligning income with expenses. It helps people and associations in understanding where their cash is coming from and where it is going, encouraging monetary discipline.

• Emergency Preparedness:

A well-crafted financial plan includes provisions for unexpected events. Crisis reserves, a critical part of monetary preparation, go about as a wellbeing net, giving monetary dependability during unexpected conditions.

• Debt Management:

Budgeting aids in managing debt effectively. Allocating funds for debt repayment within a financial plan helps individuals and businesses work towards reducing liabilities and achieving financial freedom.

• Prioritizing Spending:

Through budgeting, it becomes evident where spending priorities lie. It allows for conscious decision-making, directing resources toward high-priority areas and minimizing expenditures on non-essential items.

• Long-Term Wealth Building:

Financial planning extends beyond day-to-day expenses; it encompasses wealth-building strategies. Ventures, investment funds, and retirement arranging are fundamental components that add to long haul monetary security.

• Adaptability to Change:

Both budgeting and financial planning provide a framework that can adapt to changing circumstances. Whether facing economic fluctuations, personal life changes, or unexpected expenses, a well-structured financial plan allows for flexibility.

• Risk Mitigation:

Financial planning includes risk assessment and mitigation strategies. By differentiating ventures and having alternate courses of action set up, people and organizations can explore vulnerabilities with more noteworthy strength.

• Educational Investments:

For individuals, financial planning often involves saving for education. Whether for personal development or funding the education of children, allocating resources strategically contributes to educational aspirations.

• Business Expansion:

In the business realm, financial planning plays a crucial role in expansion strategies. It incorporates looking over capital necessities, surveying adventure open entryways, and ensuring money related practicality during advancement stages.

• Retirement Security:

A key aspect of financial planning is securing a comfortable retirement. Strategically saving and investing throughout one's career helps individuals ensure a financially secure and fulfilling retirement.

• **Tax Efficiency:**

Financial planning includes optimizing tax strategies. Understanding tax implications and employing legal strategies enable individuals and businesses to maximize their after-tax income.

• **Regular Review and Adjustment:**

Both budgeting and financial planning are dynamic processes. Standard surveys consider changes in view of evolving objectives, monetary circumstances, or individual conditions, guaranteeing progressing pertinence.

• **Empowerment and Peace of Mind:**

At last, planning and monetary arranging engage people and associations to assume command over their monetary fates. Peace of mind, reduced financial stress, and a positive relationship with money are all benefits of this sense of control.

Planning and monetary arranging are not simply managerial undertakings but rather incredible assets that engage people and organizations to shape their monetary fates, explore difficulties, and fabricate a safe and prosperous future.

Tracking expenses and revenues

Following operational expenses is a fundamental piece of being a mindful and keen entrepreneur. By following your spending, you can separate districts where you might actually save cash and further foster your pay.

Observing the two incomes and costs is a fundamental piece of viable monetary administration. This gives basic experiences into people's and affiliations' monetary circumstancesThis deliberate procedure incorporates the decided recording and advancing seeing of each and every money related trade, giving a comprehensive blueprint of inflows and floods. The careful following of these monetary perspectives is urgent for informed independent direction, vital planning, and keeping up with generally speaking monetary wellbeing.

For people, monitoring costs is the establishment for making a practical spending plan. This involves recording all uses, from fixed month to month charges like lease and utilities to variable costs like food and diversion. By classifying and investigating these consumptions, people can perceive designs, distinguish regions where expenses can be managed, and adjust their ways of managing money with explicit monetary objectives.

Conversely, revenue tracking for individuals encompasses all sources of income, offering a holistic view of financial inflows.This includes salaries, bonuses, investment returns, side hustle earnings, and any other monetary streams. Consistently tracking revenues help individuals assess their overall financial situation, plan for savings, ensure that income is sufficient to cover expenses, and contribute to the achievement of financial goals.

For organizations, fastidious following of costs and incomes is basic for monetary supportability and development. Working expenses, going from lease and utilities to pay rates and variable creation costs, are kept exhaustively. This data isn't just critical for planning yet in addition for cost control, vital navigation, and assessing the monetary attainability of tasks or extension plans.

Income following for organizations stretches out past essential marketing projections to incorporate ventures and other monetary sources. Organizations can recognize their most beneficial items or administrations, assess the viability of showcasing systems, and settle on taught choices with respect to valuing and deals procedures on account of this exhaustive following.

There are various advances and devices accessible to work on the most common way of following incomes and costs. From central computation sheets to complex accounting programming, these instruments give a proficient technique for contributing, requesting, and looking at money related data. Robotization highlights assist with lessening mistakes and save time, permitting people and organizations to zero in on more key monetary preparation.

For spotting examples and making proactive changes, ordinary and efficient audits of the cost and income reports are fundamental. This ceaseless evaluations draw in individuals to change their approaches to overseeing cash, refine spending plans, and assurance that money related targets stay both sensible and achievable. For associations, standard money related overviews add to fundamental free course, helping authority bunches fathom the financial strength of the association and go with informed choices about adventures, expansions, or cost-saving measures.

The act of following costs and incomes goes past the mechanical recording of exchanges; about acquiring significant bits of knowledge drives monetary achievement. This correspondence makes monetary consideration, empowers risk, and interfaces with people and relationships to pursue taught choices in view in regards to a reasonable comprehension of their cash related scene.

The fastidious and steady following of costs and incomes isn't simply an accounting exercise — a principal practice furnishes people and organizations with the urgent information required for informed direction, spending enhancement, and the acknowledgment of their monetary goals. The upsides of this training stretch out a long way past essential bookkeeping and contribute fundamentally to generally monetary wellbeing and flexibility, whether utilizing progressed monetary devices or keeping records physically.

Following costs of doing business is significant for keeping up with business tasks, and laying out a legitimate following strategy has many advantages, including:

Making it simpler to apportion reserves: Following operational expenses can assist you with deciding how to designate subsidies all the more effectively, including assets for movement, office supplies or worker rewards.

Working on the duty cycle: Laying out a technique for following costs of doing business can make it more straightforward to apply for a duty derivation since it permits you to list all the operational expenses in a reasonable configuration.

Smoothing out accounting works on: Following costs of doing business can be a particularly valuable method for guaranteeing exactness while making and keeping up with monetary records, which is frequently essential for accounting.

Step by step instructions to follow operational expense

The following are six stages you can use to follow costs of doing business precisely:

• Open a financial balance for business

The most important phase in following operational expense includes opening a ledger explicitly for business-related exchanges. When it comes to making payments for operational expenses like advertising and office supplies, business financial balances are invaluable. In the event that your boss doesn't as of now have a business ledger, consider empowering them to make one to help record and track expenses all the more effectively and keep away from the responsibility related with utilizing an individual financial balance for deals. It might likewise be valuable to apply for a different charge card for operational expenses.

• Select a bookkeeping framework

When you have a different business ledger, you can pick a fitting bookkeeping framework to more readily follow costs. The two essential sorts of bookkeeping frameworks are money and gathering. A gathering bookkeeping framework records income or costs as they happen, while cash bookkeeping possibly perceives exchanges when there's a trade of money. You might need to contrast these two strategies to figure out which may be best for your boss.

• Classify each cost utilizing programming

No matter what the bookkeeping framework you pick, involving business or bookkeeping programming to lay out a strategy for recording your expenses is frequently valuable. Business programming can assist you with guaranteeing that your monetary data is precise and forward-thinking while likewise improving on the recording system. You can explore online to decide the various kinds of programming accessible. A few sorts might be more helpful for bigger associations, while others might have more elements for more modest organizations. Attempt to pick programming that furnishes you with the choice to look at costs and make classes for them.

• Interface the ledger to the product

You can work on the most common way of following costs of doing business by interfacing the business financial balance to the bookkeeping programming you picked. Thus, you can more readily safeguard the organization's significant monetary information and gain extra oversight. In the wake of finishing the association, you can consequently download all deals straightforwardly to the bookkeeping programming that you picked. Laying out programmed imports can assist with guaranteeing you miss no progressions to the business account and permit you to lessen how much time you spend on accounting.

• Deal with your receipts

Make duplicates of business-related receipts to more readily oversee and monitor costs. These records can be particularly significant when now is the right time to cover charges, as they can assist you with giving verification of the need to burden derivations and discounts. There are additionally versatile applications you can use to make computerized duplicates of business receipts, which can assist you with diminishing the requirement for actual capacity. Consider putting resources into an application that permits you to connect receipts to business solicitations. A few applications might try and naturally make cost reports for reimbursable costs.

• Record and review your expenses

Record all the functional costs to ensure they're addressed, then, study them once this moment is the best opportunity to coordinate a survey. On the off chance that you finish up you would prefer not to record your costs through a modified cycle, think about placing assets into programming systems or applications that license you to enter your expenses truly. You could moreover choose to record your costs on a plan, as close to the completion of each and every little while times consistently. Endeavor to sort functional cost reliably and use them to help your bearing.

Ways of following functional cost

The following are a couple of clues to help you with following functional cost even more easily:

• Measure your money related data

Consider your continuous level of money related data and use it to sort out what kind of programming or accounting systems might be best for you. In case the association has an arrangement of business accounts and many expenses, placing assets into programming with more grouping devices could be more brilliant. If the association is close to nothing and causes relatively few expenses, direct bookkeeping sheet programming may be more useful. Despite what you pick, endeavor to review the association's expense estimations sometimes and think about techniques for chipping away at the viability of the recording framework.

• Consider enlisting a representative

Selecting a representative can help you with the following functional cost even more definitively. A representative regulates money related segments for affiliations and trains them about their trades and assets. Various representatives capability as trained professionals or on a legitimately restricting reason. They may similarly perform a lot of their work in a good way. You can examine different bookkeeping organizations online to recognize representatives that recommend rates inside your supervisor's spending plan.

• Perceive the evaluation deductible expenses

Perceive any expenses of carrying on with work that are charge deductible to conclude how the affiliation could expand its pay and saved cash. There is a grouping of obligation deductible expenses for associations. These expenses could include:

•Advancing: Publicizing could incorporate flyers, online promotions and some other mechanized or real displaying materials.

•Rent: Rent consolidates costs for procuring equipment and stuff or any additional things and property related with the business.

•**Banking charges**: Banking costs are the costs related with opening and keeping a business record.

•**Vehicles:** If the association uses vehicles, trucks, vans or one more vehicle for business, you can deduct the mileage and costs of gas.

•**Dwelling:** It's similarly possible to deduct home-related costs if the business sorts out of a home, similar to home child care associations.

•**Food:** Associations that lead business at restaurants or solicitation sustenance for delegates could have the choice to deduct business supper costs.

•**Fixes**: This integrates the costs of fixes and upkeep for business gear, like fax machines, printers, phones and copiers.

•**Travel:** In case agents travel for business reliably, the connected expenses could in like manner be deductible.

•**Agents:** The costs of specialist wages and benefits are in like manner charge deductible.

Basic accounting for small businesses

Accounting is basic for every business. Savvy record-keeping is key for actually taking a look at functional cost and tracking down new streets of improvement. Also, keeping up with exact records guarantees that entrepreneurs stay answerable for charge commitments to the public authority and their workers.

Small business accounting needs exact bookkeeping, which includes staying aware of composed records of a business' money related trades, including bargains, expenses, assets, and liabilities.

Accountants normally work with three kinds of bookkeeping reports: balance sheets, income statements and cash flow.

Balance sheet

A balance sheet measures what an organization claims and owes. This kind of assertion gives a depiction of a private company's monetary wellbeing at a particular moment. Representatives can see the association's assets and commitment figures at first.

Organizations regularly plan asset reports toward the finish of each and every quarter, except people can set them up whenever. Assets, liabilities, and shareholder equity involve a balance sheet.

Assets

Resources have monetary worth and can diminish expenses and further develop deals. Instances of resources incorporate land, stock, money, and records receivable. Accounting reports list resources arranged by liquidity — how effectively they can be sold, polished off, or transformed into cash.

Liabilities

Liabilities are something an organization owes to another person. Instances of liabilities incorporate representative wages, annual expenses, contract credits, and records payable.

Shareholders equity

Financial backers' worth tends to an association's absolute resources — the aggregate financial backers would get if they sold all assets and repaid all commitments. Total assets can likewise be perceived as resources short liabilities.

Income Statement

A small business's income and expenses over a specific time period are summarized in income statements, also known as profit and loss statements. Organizations commonly get ready quarterly and yearly pay explanations.

Income statements center around four critical things — Revenue, gains, expenses, and losses — which clerks use to compute overall gain.

Revenue and Gains

Revenue incorporates operating and non-operating revenue. The operating revenue makes up a business' essential exercises, such as selling items. Through secondary business activities like the interest on bank accounts, businesses generate non-operating revenue.

Gains incorporate cash produced using one-time, non-business exercises, such as auctioning off old hardware or unused structures.

Expenses and Losses

Expenses incorporate costs accumulated through essential and auxiliary business exercises. Essential exercises incorporate general managerial costs, innovative work, and the expense of merchandise sold.

Losses incorporate components like ominous claim settlements and resources sold for not exactly their worth.

Net income

Bookkeepers work out total compensation by deducting operating expenses from its income. Assuming income is higher than costs, the business acquires net benefit. On the off chance that income is lower than costs, the business encounters an overall deficit.

Cash Flow statement

Cash flow statements sum up how much cash enters and leaves an organization. These assertions center solely around fluid resources like endlessly cash counterparts — ventures that people can promptly transform into cash.

Adjustments to a company's income statement are used by accountants to calculate cash flow. Through expansion and deduction, accountants eliminate non-cash things and exchanges from the overall gain. Parts of an income proclamation incorporate working exercises, contributing exercises, and funding exercises.

Operating Activities

Operating activities involve the generation and expenditure of funds for business purposes. Receipts from sales of items, bank account interest, payments to suppliers, and wages paid to staff are all considered running activities by businesses.

Investing Activities

Asset sales or purchases, vendor loans, and payments associated with corporate acquisitions or mergers are all examples of investments.

Financing activities

Financing operations involve earning and spending cash to fund the business, such as paying cash dividends to shareholders, obtaining cash from stock issuance, and receiving cash from debt repayment.

Compelling monetary administration for your private company stretches out past accounting. You can effectively expect your association's future and agree to regulatory essentials by using capable accounting procedures.

At this point, successful small firms should consider either outsourcing or investing in accounting software.

Chapter 9: Scaling and Future Growth

Building a productive association is about fundamentally more than growing arrangements and pay.

While scaling a business, an association likewise needs the right methodology, group, and cycles set up to help new clients, items, and administrations.

While any business chief fantasies about turning into an unexpected phenomenon, fruitful scaling includes building and executing a long haul, practical methodology. Regardless of the size of your business, understanding scaling and recognizing significant advances you can take to do both keys to arriving at your objectives are as well.

The expressions "development" and "scale" are frequently utilized conversely. While the two are related, they have distinct differences.

Development alludes to expanding income at the very rate that a business adds assets — like new colleagues, innovation, and capital, to give some examples. Then again, scaling is the point at which an association distinguishes ways of developing all the more proficiently, bringing about income development at a significantly more prominent rate than expansions in assets and expenses.Scaling a business requires thoughtful, strategic planning.

Embarking on the journey of scaling and future growth is like orchestrating a symphony of possibilities for small businesses. Picture it: a strategic roadmap unfolds, where goals sparkle on the horizon, and the rhythm of success beats in harmony with well-crafted plans.

At the center of attention, key arranging becomes the overwhelming focus, establishing the vibe for what lies ahead. It's about defining goals with the clarity of a hit single and conducting a SWOT analysis that rocks out the strengths, tames the weaknesses, embraces opportunities, and faces threats head-on.

The crescendo forms with statistical surveying, a behind the stage pass to understanding the beat of client needs and the musicality of market patterns. This symphony requires financial preparedness — securing funding becomes the bassline, and budgeting becomes the melody, orchestrating every note of expansion.

Operational efficiency steps into the limelight as processes streamline and technology takes the lead. A scalable business model, flexible and agile, dances gracefully to the music of demand, while a talented team, the heart of the ensemble, harmonizes through continuous learning and development.

As the spotlight widens, the audience of customers takes center stage. Customer satisfaction becomes the anthem, sung with the passion of loyal patrons, and marketing strategies play like a well-tuned instrument attracting new admirers while serenading existing ones.

Broadening ventures into the spotlight, a performance act investigating new skylines in items or administrations and wandering into new geological business sectors. Technology adopts a techno beat, transforming the business into a digital symphony, with e-commerce as a dynamic refrain.

Partnerships and collaborations join the performance, creating a duet of shared success. Risk the board adds anticipation to the story by recognizing expected snags and creating systems for conquering them. Customer feedback becomes the applause, guiding the encore and influencing adaptations.

Legal and regulatory compliance provide the baseline for ethical business practices, while measuring success becomes the anthem sung by key performance indicators. Manageability rehearses add a green note, making the business a dependable player in the business' symphony.

The fabulous finale shows up with worldwide development, where the business soaks up the adoration on global stages, embracing different business sectors with social artfulness.Continuous innovation, the encore, ensures the melody of success remains fresh and resonant, a timeless tune in the business repertoire.

Networking and industry involvement become the encore, connecting the business with fellow performers and ensuring a standing ovation in the business arena. The ensemble of scaling and future development, a work of art created by essential splendor, monetary concordance, and functional creativity, leaves the crowd rooting for a reprise.

Strategies for business expansion

All successful businesses or startups ultimately face the challenge of whether they should expand their business or not. From expanding pieces of the pie and client base to diminishing expenses and further developing activities, the advantages of extension are plentiful.

Be that as it may, it is likewise loaded with risks and, in the event that is not overseen as expected, business extension can mean ruin for a striving business. It very well may be an unnerving interaction, particularly when you are not furnished with the right devices to make your business objectives a reality. When a company has reached a point of growth and is actively seeking additional opportunities to generate greater profits, it typically experiences business expansion.

Business improvement takes on different designs. It incorporates buying new resources, opening new units, adding deals workforce, expanding publicizing, adding establishments, entering new business sectors, giving new items or administrations, from there, the sky's the limit.

There are numerous inspirations driving why private associations deal with the issue of developing their commitments. One of the most widely recognized reasons referred to by specialists is the absence of assets.The presence of too few employees in a given company can be quite a deterrent to expansion efforts as they would have to spend a lot of time training new people who may not necessarily have the same skill set or expertise as those who've been working for the company for a while. Another One more component referred to by entrepreneurs is the dialing back of deals because of monetary variables.

Business people need to be aware of business-related market trends. As a matter of fact, a huge portion of new independent ventures are begun by business people who don't have a reasonable thought of what is moving and what isn't.

To extend their endeavors, a large number of these business visionaries should lead research on the thing as of now selling great on the lookout. This examination is particularly pivotal assuming that the business depends on conventional promotion like post office based mail or TV advertisements.

Before any business visionary can leave on an extension program, they should initially figure out a sound business development plan. Most business visionaries neglect to extend their endeavors infeasible from the shortfall of a sound business extension plan. Without an obvious business extension plan, an entrepreneur might wind up causing more damage than great to their organization.

The most common way of extending a business includes cautious preparation, business examination, and the utilization of monetary assets. To extend a business, ideally, let's foster a distinct vision, mission, and marketable strategy. Business people actually should figure out what sort of extension they need to do. Once not entirely settled, they can then continue to foster a reasonable business development plan.

Subsequent to fostering a business extension plan, business visionaries should figure out what steps they will take to carry out their new strategies. For instance, they might draw in the administrations of experienced experts like monetary specialists and activities organizers. These people can furnish them with itemized marketable strategies and monetary estimates. On the other hand, they can look for direction on tasks and business arranging issues by reaching business tutors.

It is vital to recognize that business extension methodologies are not a one-size-fits-all sort of arrangement. They can change and develop along with your own company's goals, objectives, and specific circumstances. These methodologies can likewise fluctuate contingent upon the sort of development you are examining. On the off chance that you are venturing into another market, for instance, the procedure you will utilize will be not quite the same as assuming you were to just grow your organization's presence to a new location. At last, it depends on you to sort out which business extension methodology will best address your organization's issues.

In view of that, here are a few methodologies for business development:

• **Market Penetration Strategy**

Market entrance is a business technique pointed toward expanding the piece of the pie of an organization's items or administrations in a specific market.

The goal is to collect how many clients who utilize the affiliation's things or associations, in this manner developing the general compensation and effectiveness of the business. This methodology normally includes focusing on a particular market portion and expanding the force of promoting endeavors to arrive at potential clients who have not yet utilized the organization's items or administrations.

Instances of market infiltration procedures incorporate contribution special limits, expanding promoting spend, growing dissemination channels, further developing item quality, or offering extra administrations to existing clients. By utilizing these techniques, organizations can really build their perceivability and appeal to likely clients, bringing about an expanded portion of the overall industry and income.

One of the fundamental advantages of this approach is that it permits organizations to use their previous items/administrations to increment deals as opposed to putting resources into item improvement. Moreover, market infiltration can likewise prompt expanded pieces of the pie while lessening your rivals' portion.

This sort of extension is appropriate for private ventures hoping to lay down a good foundation for themselves in a cutthroat market and organizations with a generally solid buyer base, as they offer a practical method for extending their client base and drive deals development.

• Marketing And Promotion

One more procedure to extend your business is to have a strong showcasing and limited time system set up to boost your portion of the overall industry. There is no one single recipe for making progress with regards to promoting, and what works for one brand may not work for the other. One methodology, in any case, is to enable your business through showcasing and special techniques that make solid client devotion to your business.

Client dedication might be accomplished through various means. Running arrangements and advancements, having a prizes framework, or cultivating major areas of strength for a media presence are only a couple of ways you can catch client dedication.

By expanding your showcasing and special endeavors, you will make major areas of strength for a picture that permits you to set up a good foundation for yourself in your industry as a prevailing power and become immediately unmistakable to buyers.

• Expansion Into A New Market

At the point when a market becomes soaked with one kind of item or administration, that market might start to evaporate. You might have seen the conventional business pattern where organizations have ventured into regions where they were beforehand unfit to carry on with work because of market immersion. This is what we refer to as market expansion. Market development alludes to the course of a business entering new business sectors or extending its reach in existing business sectors. It commonly includes extending a business' item or administration presenting as a way to advance development.

Market extension is regularly great for those that have arrived at a level in their current business sectors and are searching for new open doors for development. It is for those organizations that have effectively entered their current business sectors and have serious areas of strength for a base and brand personality are in many cases strategically set up to investigate new markets.

• **Expand Your Business Abroad**

Eventually, for organizations, the nearby market becomes immersed, and the best way to grow is to travel to another country. This is a step that many companies are afraid of because it comes with challenges, but also many opportunities because you are able to sell your products or services to more users.

Growing abroad may mean stirring up your business methodology or learning new things.

• Start A Franchise

Expanding a business through franchising can be an effective way to grow and increase revenue. At the point when a business chooses to franchise, it permits others to open and work their own area of the business under a similar brand name, working framework, and rules as the original business.

Starting a foundation offers a couple of benefits to associations. Right off the bat, it considers quick ventures into new business sectors with lower monetary gamble for the franchisor. The franchisee is answerable for supporting the new region's send off, which might lessen the franchisor's monetary weight. Likewise, it might augment at any point brand care and affirmation as the franchisee places assets into publicizing and propelling the business in their close-by market. This can eventually drive more clients to the first business and the other establishment areas.

Furthermore, diversifying gives a controlled climate in which the franchisor can keep up with steady marking and functional norms across all areas. It helps with ensuring a positive client experience and building client trustworthiness. Franchisees are additionally given preparation and support from the franchisor, which can improve the probability of their prosperity and at last add to the outcome of the whole establishment framework.

• **Enter A Joint Endeavor Or Procurement Understanding**

Going into a joint endeavor or procurement concurrence with another business can be a strong methodology for business development. In a joint venture, two or more businesses work together on a particular project or business venture, whereas in an acquisition, one business buys another.

By going into a joint endeavor or securing concurrence with a bigger, more settled business, you can get sufficiently close to their assets, including innovation, skill, and client base. This can assist with lessening the time and cost expected to grow your business into new business sectors or to foster new items or administrations.

In a joint endeavor, the two affiliations convey their magnificent assets for the connection, which can put forth a planned attempt that helps the two players. For instance, a little tech startup could collaborate with a bigger company to foster another product item, joining the startup's specialized skill with the enterprise's assets and market reach.

In a procurement, the securing business acquires responsibility for gained business and its resources. This can be a more clear method for venturing into new business sectors or enterprises rapidly, by utilizing the gained business' current client base, brand notoriety, and skill.

Planning for long-term success

Making game plans for long stretch accomplishment is a fundamental collaboration that incorporates setting clear targets, making plausible strategies, and acclimating to changing circumstances to ensure continued improvement and achievement. Whether for people, organizations, or associations, a very much created long haul plan fills in as a guide for exploring difficulties, immediately jumping all over chances, and making progress.

• Vision and Mission:

Long haul achievement starts with a convincing vision and mission. Lay out a reasonable and rousing vision for the future, illustrating what achievement resembles. The mission ought to characterize the reason and values that guide choices and activities.

• Objective Setting:

Set explicit, quantifiable, reachable, significant, and time-bound (Savvy) objectives. These objectives give a structure to long haul arranging and act as achievements to follow progress. Adjust objectives to the general vision and mission of the element.

• Key Preparation:

Foster a complete well thought out plan that frames the moves toward accomplish long haul targets. This includes dissecting qualities, shortcomings, open doors, and dangers (SWOT examination), and forming procedures that influence qualities and relieve shortcomings.

• Monetary Preparation:

Make financial planning a part of the long-term plan. This incorporates planning, speculation, arranging, and hazarding the executives. Guarantee a maintainable monetary construction that upholds development and endures financial vacillations.

• Development and Versatility:

Long haul achievement requires a promise to develop and flexibility. Be up to date with the latest industry trends, technological advancements, and customer requirements. Embrace change and be ready to likewise change procedures.

• Ability Improvement:

Put resources into ability advancement and progression arranging. Sustain a gifted and persuaded labor force, give open doors to development, and recognize potential pioneers who can direct the association towards long haul achievement.

• Putting the customer first:

Focus on consumer loyalty and reliability. Figure out client assumptions, accumulate input, and adjust items or administrations likewise. Having strong relationships with customers are important for long-term success.

• Risk Management:

Identify and assess potential risks that could impact long-term goals. Foster gamble relief methodologies to safeguard against vulnerabilities, guaranteeing flexibility despite challenges.

• Environmental and Social Responsibility:

Incorporate environmental and social responsibility into long-term planning. Consider the environmental and community effects of operations. Manageable and socially dependable practices add to long haul achievement.

• Continuous Improvement:

Foster a culture of continuous improvement. Regularly assess processes, performance, and strategies. Carry out input instruments to distinguish regions for improvement and development.

• Brand Building:

Build a strong and reputable brand. Consistently deliver quality products or services, maintain transparency, and uphold ethical standards. Success over the long term is significantly influenced by a positive brand image.

• Collaboration and Partnerships:

Seek collaborative opportunities and strategic partnerships. Building solid unions with different elements can open roads for development, asset sharing, and aggregate critical thinking.

• **Regulatory Compliance:**

Ensure compliance with relevant regulations and industry standards. Keeping up to date with lawful prerequisites mitigates the gamble of legitimate difficulties that could subvert long haul achievement.

• **Monitoring and Evaluation:**

Establish key performance indicators (KPIs) and metrics to monitor progress. Regularly evaluate performance against set goals, making adjustments as needed to stay on course for long-term success.

• **Crisis Preparedness:**

Develop contingency plans for potential crises. The company will be able to overcome obstacles without jeopardizing its long-term objectives, If it has a clearly defined crisis management strategy.

• Global Perspective:

Consider a global perspective in long-term planning, especially in an interconnected world. Evaluate worldwide market patterns, investigate global open doors, and be ready to extend past nearby limits.

• Technology Integration:

Leverage technology for efficiency and innovation. Taking on and incorporating applicable innovations upgrades activities, further develops intensity, and adds to long haul achievement.

• Customer Feedback:

Actively seek and incorporate customer feedback. Product, service, and overall business strategy refinement can benefit greatly from customer insights.

• Ethical Leadership:

Embrace ethical leadership practices. Building trust, keeping a positive hierarchical culture, and guaranteeing long haul achievement all rely upon moral navigation and uprightness.

• Flexibility and Resilience:

Cultivate flexibility and resilience as core organizational attributes. For long haul achievement, it is fundamental to have the option to acclimate to new conditions and return quickly from mishaps.

Preparing or Planning for long-term success involves a holistic and dynamic approach. It requires premonition, flexibility, and a confirmation to driving improvement. A compelling significant length course of action is a basic register extended length accomplishment for people, affiliations, or affiliations.

Conclusion: Celebrating Your Entrepreneurial Journey

All things considered, perceiving your leading experience is a pivotal and savvy cycle that includes the accomplishments, inconveniences, and improvement you've encountered as a cash chief.This celebration is more than just a time of appreciation; a critical achievement perceives the commitment, versatility, and vision that moved you along the innovative way.

Pondering Accomplishments:

Find an opportunity to commend the accomplishments, both of all shapes and sizes, that have denoted your enterprising excursion. Whether it's effectively sending off an item, getting a key organization, or outperforming monetary achievements, every accomplishment adds to the account of your innovative story.

Embracing Difficulties as Learning experiences:

Business venture is intrinsically difficult, and defeating snags is an indispensable piece of the excursion. Praise the difficulties you've confronted, recognizing them not as misfortunes but rather as any open doors for development and learning. A show of your flexibility and confirmation is in your ability to investigate difficulties.

Appreciation for the Excursion:

Offer thanks for the actual excursion. Give thanks to your team, mentors, customers, and loved ones—whoever has helped you. Business venture is regularly a collaboration, and perceiving the commitments of the people who have been a part of it is a significant piece of praising the excursion.

Gaining from Mishaps:

In the enterprising scene, misfortunes are unavoidable. Recognize your capacity to acquire from these failures and change them into supportive models that influence your philosophy and decisions. Each challenge is an astounding entryway to refine your systems and further encourage your starting degree of cutoff points.

Personal Development and Growth:

Consider the self-improvement and advancement you've encountered all through your innovative excursion. Commend the advancement of your abilities, outlook, and authority capacities. Business isn't just about building organizations; it's tied in with incorporating oneself into an additional able and tough person.

Influence on Others and the Local area:

Think about the effect your enterprising undertakings have had on others and the local area. Whether through work creation, inventive arrangements, or local area commitment, commend the positive effect you've had. Business goes past individual achievement; it has the ability to make positive change on a more extensive scale.

Versatility and Development:

Pioneering ventures are set apart by the requirement for versatility and advancement. Commend your capacity to turn, embrace change, and remain in front of market patterns. The enterprising soul flourishes with development, and your ability to advance is an estimable part of your excursion.

Putting forth New Objectives:

As you praise your enterprising excursion, think about putting forth new objectives and goals. Undertaking is a dynamic and forward-looking endeavor. Take the force from your past achievements and use it to drive yourself higher than ever and investigate new open doors.

Energizing Others:

Your spearheading adventure is a wellspring of inspiration for others, whether developing business visionaries or those searching for motivation in their employment. Commend the valuable chance to share your story, experiences, and examples got the hang of, adding to the aggregate information and motivation inside the pioneering local area.

Enjoying the Spirit of Entrepreneurship:

Above all else, give credit to your entrepreneurial spirit for initiating this journey. The mental fortitude to seek after your vision, face challenges, and continue even with difficulties is a surprising quality. Relish the quintessence of business venture, embracing the energy and assurance that powers your undertakings.

For the most part, commending your spearheading adventure is a depiction of appreciation for the different weaving of experiences, improvement, and impact that portray your direction. Push ahead, setting out new open doors and making a permanent imprint on the pioneering scene, since you know about your enterprising soul.

Reflecting on achievements

Pondering achievements is a critical practice that invites individuals to mindfully see the worth in the accomplishments they have shown up in both individual and master circles. It transcends clear accreditation; it cultivates a basic energy of appreciation, care, and motivation for future endeavors. First and foremost, developing appreciation turns into a characteristic result of considering accomplishments, empowering people to perceive the help, open doors, and conditions that added to their prosperity. It pushes a moving viewpoint and an impression of interconnectedness.

What's more, mulling over achievements licenses people to notice and cheer proficient and self-awareness. Individuals gain understanding into how issues, encounters, and learning open entryways have outlined them all in all by following their excursion through past triumphs. This verification of progress changes into an establishment for building conviction and sureness, shaping the bedrock for future achievements. Helping certainty is the third viewpoint, as returning to past triumphs fills in as a sign of one's capacities, versatility, and ability to beat difficulties, adding to a more engaged identity.

Besides, pondering accomplishments fills in as a persuasive device, reigniting the flash that drives people forward. Also It assists them with recalling their ability to advance targets, work consistently, and achieve positive outcomes.

This inspirational lift becomes urgent for keeping up with energy and setting new yearnings, denoting the fourth point.The fifth step is to identify one's strengths because accomplishments frequently highlight an individual's strengths and abilities. It awards people the chance to notice and integrate these attributes into resulting attempts, in this manner expanding kept up with accomplishment.

Learning from challenges constitutes the sixth aspect of reflecting on achievements. Having an understanding of how tangles were crushed gives significant pieces of information into adaptability, decisive abilities to reason, and adaptability, developing relentless learning. Setting new goals is the seventh point; the reflective process becomes an opportune time to identify areas for further growth and to establish challenging yet achievable objectives. This forward-looking methodology guarantees a nonstop pattern of individual and expert turn of events.

Furthermore, reflecting on achievements fosters self-awareness as the eighth element. A more significant understanding of their characteristics, motivations, and areas of energy are gained by individuals. Care is instrumental in settling on informed choices concurred with individual and expert goals. Encouraging a positive outlook is the 10th perspective, as commending accomplishments moves the concentration from difficulties and misfortunes to achievements and triumphs. An elevating viewpoint changes into a critical resource in researching future undertakings.

Taking into account achievements is a remarkable practice that loosens up past the basic affirmation of past victories.Through developing appreciation, recognizing development, helping certainty, persuading positive progress, distinguishing qualities, gaining from difficulties, defining new objectives, encouraging mindfulness, and advancing a positive mentality, people leave on a powerful cycle that drives them toward proceeded with development and makes way for very interesting yearnings.

Encouragement for the road ahead

As you set out on the unique way of business venture, pause for a minute to perceive the boldness inside you. Beginning a business isn't only an endeavor; it's an excursion of self-revelation, strength, and steady assurance. When faced with challenges, view them not as roadblocks but as stepping stones toward your ultimate goal.

In the face of uncertainty, let encouragement be your guiding star. Embrace the unavoidable difficulties as significant examples that shape your enterprising intuition. Your flexibility and fortitude are demonstrated with each obstacle you surmount. Keep in mind, the street ahead might be twisting, however every diversion presents a chance for development and refinement.

Fuel your journey with passion, for it is the driving force that propels you through the inevitable highs and lows. Passion transforms obstacles into mere detours on the path to success. Cultivate a mindset that sees challenges as invitations to innovate and overcome. Draw nearer to comprehending your vision as you conquer every obstacle.

Constancy is your most prominent partner. As you encounter setbacks, let them be a source of motivation rather than discouragement. Perseverance is the foundation of lasting success. True entrepreneurs stand out from the crowd because they are able to rise from adversity despite each setback

Gratify your successes, no matter how small they may be. It's barely noticeable the meaning of steady advancement while putting forth grandiose objectives. Recognize and relish every accomplishment, as they on the whole add to the account of your prosperity.

In snapshots of uncertainty, ponder the underlying flash that touched off your enterprising excursion.That passion, that unwavering belief in your vision—let them be your compass. Trust in your capacities will bring you through vulnerabilities and impart trust in the people who go along with you on this extraordinary endeavor.

As you explore the road ahead, recollect that each challenge is a chance to refine your methodology and develop as a business visionary.The compass that guides you in the correct heading is your responsibility, and the excursion is similarly pretty much as significant as the objective.

You are not merely starting a business; you are crafting a legacy. The road ahead may request your best, however with each step, you shape a story of flexibility, energy, and unflinching assurance. Embrace the excursion, for inside it lies the substance of your enterprising victory You've got the vision, the passion, and the perseverance—forge ahead with confidence, and success will undoubtedly be your companion.

Review page

Dear Reader,

Trust this message finds you. I hope you've had the chance to explore and engage with the content in Starting a Business Guide for Beginners in 2024: Starting Strong as an Entrepreneur , Building and Sustaining a Successful Company with Ease and Confidence. Your obligation to learning and development is genuinely estimable, and I'm anxious to find out about your involvement in the book.

Your experiences are priceless, and I would extraordinarily see the value in it in the event that you could pause for a minute to share your contemplations through a survey. Whether it's featuring angles you viewed as accommodating, proposing enhancements, or sharing what the book has meant for your viewpoint, your criticism will contribute essentially to the continuous refinement of the substance.

To leave a review, simply visit the Amazon platform and locate the review section for Starting a Business Guide for Beginners in 2024: Starting Strong as an Entrepreneur, Building and Sustaining a Successful Company with Ease and Confidence. Your fair criticism won't just help me in upgrading future versions yet additionally give direction to individual perusers who are thinking about leaving on their enterprising excursion.

Much obliged to you for your time and thought. I genuinely respect the huge chance to be a piece of your strong evaluation, and your assistance means the world to me.

Wishing you proceeded with progress on your business tries!

Warm regards,

Daryl V. Meyer